LIVY'S HISTORY OF

ROME

BOOK THREE

TITUS LIVIUS
LUCAS WAGNER

Contents

INTRODUCTION

TITUS LIVIUS' GROUNDBREAKING SERIES *Ab Urbe Condita,* known as the "History of Rome" in the English-speaking world, details the founding of Rome and the establishment of the Roman Republic, covering the years 753 BC through 167 BC.

Livy's life overlapped the lives of Jesus Christ and the Emperor Augustus. Just as descriptions of their works had to be recopied by hand over many generations of humans, so too did Livy's. Most of his work did not survive the journey. Today, of the 142 original books in Ab Urbe Condita, only 35 books have survived. The books that remain contain lessons that have outlasted governments, cultures, and entire civilizations.

The sources Livy used to write his history are largely lost. In fact, for some historical events, Livy represents our only surviving record.

As Livy says in his Preface, he wrote these things down because he believed that human civilization is cyclical, calling these stories "shining memorials" which can be used by people in the future. The political philosopher Niccolò Machiavelli agreed, observing that Livy's first ten books allow us to see the impact of decisions, good and bad, across many generations of human civilization. We see patterns and cycles of power, leadership, and behavior. These broad cycles, when studied, allow us to anticipate the future. As Cicero once said, history *is* the teacher of life.

I find that reading Livy is a journey that changes people, both privately and as a citizen of a republic. A fresh understanding of how incredibly difficult and violent it is to create a stable and capable republic will change you as a leader, whether you lead people today or not. The journey has been called many things. Shocking. Uplifting. Funny. Boring. Exciting. Violent. Relatable. Tedious. Powerful. All these descriptions are true.

This version is the first 21st century translation and it follows the conventions of English as spoken in our time. In quoted dialogue, characters speak as they would speak today. Livy, when compared to the translation of Benjamin Foster over 100 years ago, speaks much more informally. We use common contractions (e.g., "don't") that readers expect. That said, we still skip uncommon or archaic ones (e.g., "'twas"). Ornate and verbose English language habits of the 19th and 20th centuries have been stripped away so that the underlying Latin is clearer.

Above all, this work is designed to be accessible and for people to enjoy. To do this, sometimes we need to add to the work. I have written chapter titles and subtitles for you to enjoy, to jog your memory, and to make it possible to "fall forward" and skip to the next subtitle. In Book I, Livy included so many names and places that, at least in the public domain versions, people can tend to quit reading before the best stories even begin. In this version, I want to help you keep moving so that you can finish the book. Fall forward to the next subtitle, but do not quit.

As Machiavelli says, while many tend to believe their state will live forever, all governments have a shelf life. Tyrants quickly rise from the perpetual fires of ailing republics. Nowhere is this clearer than in the struggles of the early Romans. Livy's story is a very human one, and it is one that continues to present day.

Lucas C. Wagner

1 November 2024

Chapter 1

DISLOYALTY OF A NEW COLONY (467-464 BC)

I. AFTER ANTIUM WAS captured, Titus Aemilius and Quintus Fabius were chosen as consuls. This Quintus Fabius was the lone survivor after the massacre at Cremera destroyed the rest of his family.

In his previous term, Consul Aemilius had advocated for distributing land that had been captured to the plebeians. So, in his second term, those who supported this idea, the so-called Agrarian Law, were hopeful that it would be passed. The tribunes pursued the matter, believing that now they could achieve their goal with the support of at least one consul. Aemilius remained unchanged in his beliefs. The landowners and a significant portion of the patricians complained that Consul Aemilius, as the state's leader, was acting like a tribune trying to grow his popularity by distributing others' property. This shifted the blame for the entire situation from the tribunes to the consul.

A COMPROMISE, A NEW COLONY

A fierce dispute grew, but Consul Fabius resolved the issue in a way that was acceptable to both sides: a large quantity of land was taken from the Volscians under the leadership of Titus Quinctius Capitolinus the previous year. This land could be used to establish a colony at Antium, which, as a seaport town not far from Rome, was a suitable city for the purpose. The plebeians could take over farms without causing the landholders to complain and the state could remain peaceful.

This plan was accepted. Fabius appointed Titus Quinctius, Aulus Verginius, and Publius Furius as triumvirs to distribute the land. Those who wanted land were instructed to register their names. However, the implementation of the plan led to dissatisfaction, as is often the case. So few plebeians registered that Volscian colonists were added to make up the numbers. The majority of the plebeians preferred to demand land inside Rome rather than accept it on the fringes of the Republic.

Also this year, the Aequians asked Consul Fabius for peace (he was sent there with an army), but the Aequians themselves violated it by suddenly invading the Latin territory.

466 BC — FIRST SIGNS OF EPIDEMIC

2. In the next year, Quintus Servilius, who was consul with Spurius Posthumius, was dispatched to confront the Aequians. He established his camp in the Latin territory.

Due to an epidemic, the army was ordered to stay within the camp.

465 BC — TAUNTING THE ROMANS

The conflict extended into the third year, with Quintus Fabius Vibulanus, for the second time, and Titus Quinctius Capitolinus Barbatus, for the third time, as consuls.

Consul Fabius was given the province by a special commission because, as the previous victor, he had granted peace to the Aequians. He was confident that his reputation would compel the Aequians to surrender, so he sent ambassadors to their council, instructing them to say that Quintus Fabius had previously brought peace to Rome from the Aequians, and now he will bring war from Rome to the Aequians. As the gods are now witnesses to their treachery and deceit, they'll soon punish those who have broken their promises. And yet, he wishes that the Aequians would repent voluntarily rather than endure the anger of an enemy. If the Aequians repent, they could rely on the same mercy they had previously experienced. If the Aequians continue to break their promises, they'll be at war with angry gods rather than their earthly enemies. However, this message had little impact on the Aequians and the ambassadors were almost assaulted.

An Aequian army was dispatched to Algidum to confront the Romans. When this news reached Rome, the insult of the situation, rather than the danger, drove Consul Quinctius to leave the City. The two consular armies advanced against the enemy in battle formation, ready to engage immediately. However, as the day was ending and no fighting had occurred, a soldier from the Aequians' front line taunted the Romans, "This is a display, Romans, not a war. You drew up your battleline when night is about to fall. We need more hours of daylight for the battle. Tomorrow at sunrise, form your battleline again. Don't worry; there will be plenty of opportunity for fighting."

Infuriated, the Roman soldiers returned to their camp to wait until the next day. They found the approaching night tedious, as it delayed the impending battle. Still, they refreshed themselves with food and sleep. At dawn, the Romans were the first to take their positions on the battlefield and wait for the Aequians. Finally, the Aequians appeared, as well.

The battle was fierce on both sides. The Romans fought with resentment and hatred, while the Aequians, aware that this was their own fault and despairing of ever being trusted again, were forced to make desperate efforts. Yet the Aequians couldn't withstand the Roman troops.

THE AEQUIANS KNOW THEIR OWN WEAKNESS

When the Aequians retreated to their own territories, their angry soldiers, still unwilling to make peace, criticized their leadership. They argued, "Our interests have been risked in one formal battle, the kind of combat in which the Romans excelled. We're better suited for raids and invasions. Smaller groups operating in different directions would wage war more effectively than one large, unwieldy army."

3. After leaving a guard at their camp, the Aequians set out and attacked the Roman territory with such intensity that it caused fear even in the City. The surprise of the attack caused even more alarm, as no one expected that a defeated enemy, almost trapped in their camp, would even think of raiding. Frightened farmers poured through the City gates, shouting with exaggeration that it wasn't just a simple raid, nor small groups of raiders, but entire armies and legions of the enemy were advancing straight for the City, ready to attack. Those who were closest to the gates spread the news, exaggerating even more what they heard from the farmers, even though it was uncertain and therefore more alarming. The rush and confused noise of those calling for defense was like the panic of a city under attack.

By chance, Consul Quinctius had just returned to Rome from Algidum, which helped to calm their fears. After quieting the chaos and scolding them for fearing a defeated enemy, he placed guards at the gates. The Senate was called into session and a general suspension of business was passed. The Consul then set out to defend the borders, leaving former consul Quintus Servilius in charge of the City, however, He found no enemy in the countryside.

Consul Fabius had great success attacking the Aequians where he knew they would be: weighed down with plundered Roman loot and moving slowly. This made their raid fatal for them. Few of the Aequians escaped the ambush and all the stolen goods were recovered.

The return of Consul Quinctius to the City ended the state of emergency and the suspension of business, which had lasted only four days. A census was then taken, and the *lustrum*, the purification ceremony performed at the end of the census, was performed by Consul Quinctius. The number of citizens counted was said to be one-hundred four thousand, seven hundred and four people, not including the orphans and widows.

Nothing notable happened afterward among the Aequians; they retreated into their towns, allowing their property to be destroyed and raided. Consul Fabius, after marching through their territory multiple times, laying waste to it with hostile intent, returned to Rome to high praise and a large amount of plunder.

464 BC — THEY LEFT MORE SUSPICIOUS THAN THEY ARRIVED

4. Aulus Posthumius Albus and Spurius Furius Fusus next became consuls. Some historians have written Furii as Fusii. I mention this to avoid confusion, as the change is only in the names, not the individuals.

From the beginning, it was clear that one of the consuls would start a war with the Aequians. The Aequians knew this and they sought help from the Volscians of Ecetra. The Volscians agreed, driven by their deep-seated hate for the Romans, and the two armies began preparing for war. The Hernician allies found out about this new alliance and warned the Romans that Ecetra had joined a revolt with the Aequians.

The Romans suspected that the colonists from the recently founded colony of Antium were disloyal. When the town was captured, many of its original inhabitants fled to the Aequians. These same Antium refugees turned out to be the bravest soldiers in the war against the Romans. After the Aequians were driven back into the walls of their towns, the Antium refugees secretly returned to Antium. Once they arrived, refugees found the colonists already alienated, and they succeeded in completely turning them against Rome.

When the Senate heard about this defection, the consuls were ordered to investigate. They summoned the colony's leaders to Rome and, while the leaders did answer the Senate's questions, they did so in such a way that made them seem even more suspicious than when they arrived. At that point, war seemed inevitable.

Consul Furius marched against the Aequians and found them raiding the Hernicians' land. He underestimated their numbers and foolishly engaged them in battle, only to be forced to retreat back to the Roman camp. The danger didn't end there, as his camp was attacked relentlessly from then on, night and day, making it impossible to send a messenger to Rome.

The Hernicians reported the news of the defeat and the blockade to the Senate. It caused such alarm that a decree was passed that Consul Posthumius should be given emergency dictatorial powers to protect the republic. It was decided that Consul Posthumius should stay in Rome to recruit more soldiers, while former consul Titus Quinctius would be sent as *pro consul*, a representative of the current consul serving as a general, to relieve the besieged camp with an army of Latins and Hernicians allies, as well as the colony of Antium, which had also been ordered to provide Quinctius with auxiliary soldiers.

WAR AGAINST THE AEQUIANS

5. During this period, many strategies and attempts were made by both sides.

The enemy, having more soldiers, tried to wear down the Roman forces by dividing them into smaller groups. They believed that the smaller forces of Romans wouldn't be able to cope with multiple attacks. The enemy blockaded the Roman camp and sent part of their army to destroy Roman lands and possibly make an attempt on the City itself, if fortune allowed.

Former consul Lucius Valerius was left to protect the City, while Consul Postumius was sent to defend the borders. There was no relaxation of vigilance or activity. Guards were stationed at the gates and posted along the walls. The suspension of courts and businesses was maintained for several days and a state of emergency was declared.

Meanwhile, Consul Spurius Furius, who had initially endured the siege in his camp, caught the Aequians off guard near the west gate on the opposite side of camp, launching a successful surprise attack. He could have continued chasing them, but he feared the majority of the enemy soldiers would enter the camp from the east side.

The consul's brother, Lieutenant General Publius Furius, was so eager to fight that he did chase the Aequians. In doing so, he didn't notice his own allies had retreated behind him and now the enemy was closing in from the rear. It was too late. His retreat path blocked, he was now trapped. The Consul's brother fought courageously, however, and after several failed attempts to return to camp, he was killed in battle. Consul Furius, upon hearing his brother was surrounded, plunged into the midst of the battle and was also wounded. He was governed more by emotion than prudence, and his men had to rescue him. The ordeal demoralized the Roman troops.

The enemy was galvanized by both the death of the lieutenant general and the consul's injury. They became bold, believing that victory was inevitable. The Romans were beaten back into their camp and were now under siege again, except, this time, they were weak and had lost hope. The situation would have been dire if pro consul Titus Quinctius hadn't arrived with reinforcements from the Latins, Hernicians, and Antium.

A DEADLY SLIP OF ATTENTION

Quinctius arrived to find the Aequian army so focused on the Roman camp that they weren't paying attention to anything else. They hadn't noticed their arrival. He glanced at the decapitated head of the fallen Roman lieutenant general prominently on display.

Immediately, he gave the signal to attack from the rear. He then gave another signal from far away so that the Romans in the camp knew to pour out of the gates. A large amount of Aequians were now surrounded on all sides by the Romans.

In other parts of Roman territory, the enemy forces weren't so much killed as scattered. As the Aequians were running and looting in different directions, Consul Postumius hit them at various points where he had previously garrisoned troops and gathered up their spoils. The fleeing enemy troops also ran into the victorious Quinctius as he was returning with the injured Consul Spurius Furius. The Roman army then avenged Consul Furius' injury and the death of Lieutenant General Publius Furius by attacking them. Both sides suffered heavy losses.

It's hard to determine the exact number of soldiers who fought or died due to how long ago this happened. However, Antias Valerius estimates that five thousand eight hundred Romans died in the Hernician territory. He also estimates that two thousand four hundred of the enemy's looting parties were killed by Consul Postumius on the Roman borders. The rest of the enemy forces who were looting, ran into Quinctius and suffered heavier losses, with four thousand two hundred thirty killed.

After this, the Romans returned to Rome and the state of emergency was lifted. In the following days, there were reports of the sky appearing to be on fire and other strange occurrences. To calm these fears, a three-day religious festival was declared, and the temples filled with people praying for the gods' protection. The Latin and Hernician cohorts after being thanked by the Senate, were dismissed and sent back home. The thousand soldiers from Antium arrived too late to help in the battle, so they were dismissed almost in disgrace.

Chapter 2
EPIDEMIC (463-462 BC)

463 BC — OUTBREAK

6. THE ELECTIONS TOOK place, and Lucius Aebutius Helva and Publius Servilius Priscus were chosen as consuls. The consuls began their term on the first day of August, which was seen as the start of the year.

This was a difficult period. The City and countryside were plagued by a deadly disease that affected both people and livestock. The situation worsened when leaders allowed the animals and farmers into the City whenever there was fear of pillaging by enemies. This influx of various animals and people led to a foul smell and overcrowded living conditions, while the country people, being packed into narrow quarters, suffered greatly from the heat and lack of sleep. Helping and caring for others, or even just coming into contact with them, spread the infection.

While struggling with these hardships, ambassadors from the Hernician allies arrived with news. The Aequians and Volscians had joined forces and set up camp in their territory, threatening their borders with a large army. The depleted Senate who showed up to hear the Hernicians made it clear that Rome was severely weakened by disease. The ambassadors received word that the outbreak was so bad that they, along with the Latin allies, would now need to defend their lands by themselves, without any assistance from Rome. Whenever the City, now too ravaged by the anger of the gods, received a respite from this disaster, Rome would provide aid just as they had done in the past. The allies left with more distressing news than what they had brought. They now had to face a war on their own, a war they had barely managed to fight even with Rome's powerful support.

The enemy didn't limit their attacks to the Hernician territory but moved into the Roman territories. They discovered Roman farms and crops were already in ruins, even without war. Their armies encountered no resistance, not even from unarmed civilians, and they reached as far as the third stone on the Gabinian Way.

Consul Aebutius died. His colleague, Consul Servilius, was barely clinging to life. Most of the influential men, most of the patricians, and all men of military age were sick. There wasn't enough strength for the necessary military operations, let alone for maintaining security. Senators who were healthy and able enough took on the role of guards. The plebeian *aediles*, elected civic magistrates, were tasked with overseeing these duties; into their hands fell the supreme control and the authority of the consuls.

"WHY WASTE TIME IN A BARREN LAND?"

7. Rome was in a state of despair. Without a leader. Without strength. However, the City's guardian gods and good fortune intervened, as they influenced the Volscians and Aequians to start considering themselves as raiders searching for loot rather than soldiers on a military conquest.

They had no hope of capturing or even approaching the walls of Rome. The sight of the distant houses and nearby hills distracted them from such an attempt. Complaints spread throughout the enemy camps, questioning why they should waste time in a barren land, amidst the rotting remains of cattle and humans, when they could go to places untouched and unspoiled by disease, like the wealthy Tusculan territory. The enemy quickly packed up their standards and traveled by crossroads through the Labicum territory to the Tusculan Hills. This is where the full force of the war was directed.

Meanwhile, the Hernicians and Latin allies, driven by both compassion and shame, decided to help. The allies felt guilty for not opposing Rome's enemy and aiding when the City was under siege. They marched to Rome with their combined forces. When the allies didn't find the enemy there, they followed rumors of their whereabouts and encountered them coming down from the Tusculan Hills into the valley of Alba. A battle ensued, but the circumstances weren't in their favor. The Hernician and Latin allies suffered heavy losses.

Back in Rome, the death toll from disease was just as high as the allies' losses in battle. The only remaining consul, Consul Servilius, died, along with other notable figures like Marcus Valerius and Titus Verginius Rutilus, the *augurs* (priests who watched birds for omens), and Servius Sulpicius, the *curio maximus* (head priest presiding over religious affairs). The disease spread widely, even among those of lower status.

The Senate, without any options left, directed the people to turn to the gods and to prayer. They were instructed to go and beg for divine protection with their wives and children. The public authority's call to do as much as each person could do, while acknowledging their own personal sufferings, led everyone to fill all the shrines. Women prostrated themselves in every temple, sweeping the floors with their hair, begging for the gods to end their anger and the plague.

462 BC — STRONG ENOUGH TO DEFEND, AND ATTACK

8. From this point, it could have been due to the favor of the gods or due to the passing of the unhealthy season, but the people's health began to improve. The Romans had overcome disease and started to focus on public matters again.

After two *interregna*, the time between reigns, had passed, Publius Valerius Publicola, three days into his role as *interrex*, a ruler between kings, facilitated the election of Lucius Lucretius Tricipitinus and Titus Veturius Geminus (or Velusius) as consuls. The consuls assumed their roles on the eleventh of August. The state was now strong enough to not only defend against attacks but also to initiate them.

When the Hernician allies reported enemy incursions into their borders, help was quickly promised by Rome. Two consular armies were formed. Consul Veturius and his army were dispatched to wage an offensive war against the Volscians. During that war, he defeated the Volscians and drove them off with only one battle. Consul Lucretius was tasked with defense, protecting the allies' territory from damage or looting. He didn't venture beyond the Hernician lands.

A group of Aequians and Volscians who had been driven off by Veturius had crossed the Praenestine Mountains, descending into the plains. The group also managed to evade Consul Lucretius' defensive watch while he was encamped among the Hernician allies. This group ravaged the fields around Praeneste and Gabii, laying waste to them, then moved toward the hills above Tusculum. This caused great alarm in Rome, more due to the suddenness of the event than a lack of strength to resist. Quintus Fabius, the former consul who was in command of the City, ensured security and tranquility by arming the young men and setting up guards. The Aequians and Volscians, not daring to approach Rome, instead looted the surrounding areas and retreated by a roundabout route.

As the Aequians and Volscians moved further away, Rome's caution and anxiety became less. However, the enemy encountered Consul Lucretius, who, though they had gotten past his defense the first time, had been tracking their line of march. He was eager to fight. Despite being outnumbered, Consul Lucretius' forces attacked with determination, causing panic among the enemy. The Romans drove them into deep valleys and surrounded them. The Volscian nation was almost entirely wiped out. Some histories record that thirteen-thousand four-hundred-seventy soldiers fell in the field. During the pursuit, one thousand seven-hundred fifty were captured alive and twenty-seven military standards were taken. Even if these numbers are exaggerated, the slaughter was nonetheless significant.

Victorious, Consul Lucretius returned to the permanent camp with an immense haul of loot. The consuls then combined their camps together. Likewise, the Volscians and Aequians also consolidated their shattered forces. The ensuing battle of consolidated forces was the third battle of that year, and the Romans were victorious again. Fortune bestowed the victory where she had done before. The enemy was so badly routed that the Aequians and Volscians even lost their camp.

Chapter 3

THE TERENTILLIAN
LAW (462-461 BC)

462 BC — FIGHTING ABUSE BY THE CONSULS

9. THE SITUATION IN Rome returned to its previous state, and successes in war immediately caused unrest in the City. Caius Terentillus Harsa (or Arsa) was tribune of the plebeians that year. He saw an opportunity for political maneuvering during the consuls' absence.

For several days, Terentillus publicly criticized the patricians' arrogance, focusing mainly on the excessive and unbearable power of the consuls' authority in a free state. Although the consuls' authority was less offensive in theory, in reality, their authority was even more oppressive than a king's. Two leaders were chosen instead of just one, and both had unrestrained, infinite power. This meant that consuls, unbounded and unchecked, tended to direct all the harshness of the law and all forms of severity against the plebeians.

To prevent this unchecked power from continuing indefinitely, Terentillus proposed a law to appoint five people to draft laws regarding consular power. The consuls should only use the power that the people granted them, and the consuls shouldn't make their own laws based on their own lust and unchecked behavior.

When this *Terentillian Law* was announced, the senators immediately became fearful that they would be subjected to oppression in the absence of the consuls, so Quintus Fabius, former consul now City prefect, called them into session. He spoke so strongly against the bill and its author, that the threats and intimidation couldn't have been greater even if the two consuls had been standing by Terentillus, threatening his life.

Fabius accused the tribune of being an opportunist and seizing upon an opportunity to attack the state. If the City had a tribune like him the previous year, during the plague and war, it would have been disastrous. Finding both consuls dead, the citizens stricken with disease, and confusion everywhere, Terentillus would have proposed a law to do away with the consular government, and it would have definitely led the Volscians and the Aequians to lay siege to the City. Was this what he wanted? Was it not enough that consuls who acted cruelly against any citizen could be brought up on charges in court by the tribunes? After all, the tribunes had the power to set a trial date for consuls. The tribunes had the power to bring the consul before the very judges whom the consul may have mistreated. It wasn't the consular authority but tribunal power that was becoming hateful and unbearable. Tribunal power, which had been peaceful and reconciled with the Senate, was about to return to its former, evil ways.

Fabius stopped pleading with Terentillus to stop his actions and addressed the tribunes as a group. "It's to you other tribunes," he cried, "whom I ask to reflect upon this fact: your power was conferred on you for the purpose of assisting individual citizens, not to ruin us all. You were elected tribunes of the people, not enemies of the senators."

"It's a source of sorrow to us and it tarnishes your reputation that the state, weakened and without its consuls, should be attacked. It'll not be seen as diminishing your authority but instead it will diminish the hate against you if you plead with your colleague to postpone the question, as it stands, until the consuls return. Even the Aequians

and the Volscians, last year, when disease had carried off the consuls, refrained from pressing a cruel and pitiless war against us."

The tribunes spoke with Terentillus, and the bill, which
seemed to be postponed, was abandoned. The consuls were immediately called back.

10. Consul Lucretius came back with a lot of spoils but even
more renown. He then increased his fame by showing off all the
spoils in the Campus Martius for three days so that every citizen
could identify and take their belongings. The rest was sold.

Everyone agreed that the Consul deserved a triumph, but it
was delayed because of the law the tribune was pushing; dealing
with this law seemed more important to Lucretius. The issue was
debated for several days in the Senate and among the plebeians.
Finally, the tribune gave in to Lucretius and stopped pushing.
Lucretius and his army were honored with a triumph, celebrating
his victory over the Volscians and Aequians. His troops followed
him in the triumph. The other consul, Veturius, was allowed to
enter Rome in an *ovation* without his soldiers.

461 BC — A TALKING COW, OR A DIVERSION?

The next year, the Terentillian Law was brought up again. This
time, it was brought up by the entire college of tribunes and
targeted the new consuls, Publius Volumnius Amintinus Gallus
and Servius Sulpicius Camerinus Cornutus.

There were signs of trouble during this year. The sky seemed to be
on fire and there was a big earthquake. People believed that a cow had
spoken. This particular rumor was determined to be too ridiculous to
be believed the year before, but the people now believed it. Among
other reported signs was a rain of flesh that a vast number of hungry

birds intercepted mid-air as they flew around. The flesh that remained scattered on the ground stayed for several days without smelling bad.

In response, the Sibylline Books were consulted by the *duumviri sacrorum,* the two magistrates for sacred rites. The predictions given to them were that there would be danger from a gathering of strangers, attacks on the highest points of Rome, and bloodshed. The duumviri also warned that all internal conflicts should be stopped.

The tribunes claimed that these frivolous issues were being prioritized in order to block the Terentillian Law, and that a big fight was coming.

A "Sham War" by the Patricians

Unsurprisingly, such that the same cycle of events might recur each year, a report then came in from the Hernician allies that the Volscians and Aequians, despite having sustained heavy losses, were rebuilding their armies. The Hernicians said that Antium was the center of support for these armies. The people of Antium were openly holding meetings at Ecetra and this, they believed, was the source and strength of the war. When the Senate heard this, they ordered a draft and told the consuls to divide the war management between them. One would handle the Volscians and the other the Aequians.

The tribunes protested in the Forum arguing that the Volscian war was a sham and the Hernicians were just playing along. The Romans' freedom was being undermined not by force, but by trickery. New enemies were being sought because it was highly unlikely that the Volscians and Aequians, having been very close to being entirely wiped out, could start a war on their own. The consuls were defaming a loyal colony near Rome and were declaring war on the innocent people of Antium. Instead, the real war was against the plebeians of Rome, now being loaded up with weapons and ushered hurriedly out of the City. This was a way for the Senate to get back at the tribunes by exile and banishment, defeating the Terentillian Law. However, while they still could, while they were still at home and in their togas, the plebeians should take care not to be driven from the City or be subject to the draft. If they had the will, help wouldn't be lacking; all the tribunes agreed. There was no external threat, no danger from abroad. The gods had made sure the previous year that their freedom could now be defended safely. All of these arguments were said by the tribunes.

11. However, the consuls, who had intentionally placed their chairs within sight of the tribunes, continued to draft soldiers for the upcoming war. The tribunes quickly hurried toward them, bringing the assembly of plebeians with them. A few of these plebeians were called to be drafted, as an experiment, and immediately, violence broke out. Whomever the *lictors* grabbed, under the consuls' orders, the tribunes then ordered to be released. There were no boundaries to anyone's authority, and whatever the consuls wanted, they tried to achieve through force.

The tribunes worked to obstruct the draft just as the consuls worked to obstruct the Terentillian Law, which was discussed every assembly day. An uproar began when the tribunes ordered the plebeians to vote but the patricians refused to leave, blocking an orderly setup for the vote. The older citizens barely participated in the conflict, as it seemed to be driven not by wisdom, but by emotion and recklessness. The consuls also generally stayed away to avoid any insult to their dignity in the chaos.

Chapter 4

A PATRICIAN BULLY (461 BC)

CAESO QUINCTIUS

THERE WAS A YOUNG patrician, Caeso, from the Quinctius family who was bold both because of his noble lineage and his physical size and strength. He had earned many military honors and was eloquent in the Forum. No one in the state was considered more effective in speech or action. When he stood in the middle of a group of patricians, he was noticeable above the rest. Because his eloquence and physical strength seemed to combine the powers of a dictator and a consul, he often alone stood against the tribunes' attacks and the plebeians' fury. He frequently took the lead in driving out the tribunes from the Forum and in causing the plebeians to scatter. Anybody who stood in his way was fined or left stripped and beaten. It became clear that if he continued this way, the Terentillian Law would be defeated.

Aulus Verginius, one of the tribunes, brought a capital charge against Caeso for his outrageous behavior. Instead of becoming intimidated, this inflamed Caeso and made him even more aggressive. He fought against the Terentillian Law more fiercely, annoyed the plebeians, and harassed the tribunes. Verginius let Caeso continue his reckless behavior not just because it added to the charges against him, but that it also stirred up public anger toward the patricians. Virginius continued to promote the Terentillian Law, not so much with the hope of passing it, but just to provoke Caeso and make him become even more reckless. Many of the younger patricians' thoughtless words and actions were now being blamed on Caeso, which only strengthened the case against him. Still, the Terentillian Law was resisted.

Verginius asked the plebeians, "Do you now realize that you can't have Caeso as a fellow citizen with the Terentillian Law you want? Why do I even mention law; Caeso is against your freedom. He's more arrogant than all the Tarquins. You already see him acting like a king over you with his strength and audacity. Just wait until he becomes a consul or dictator!" Many agreed, complaining that they had been beaten by him, and strongly encouraged Verginius to continue prosecuting Caeso.

PLEAS FOR MERCY

12. As the trial date neared, it was clear that the plebeians generally felt their freedom hinged on convicting and punishing Caeso. At last, Caeso was compelled to speak to gain the support of individual plebeians, though he did so with a sense of resentment. His family members, who were prominent figures in the state, supported him. Titus Quinctius Capitolinus Barbatus, a three-time consul, spoke of his own and his family's notable accomplishments. He claimed that there had never been such a promising young man with bravery so young in either the Quinctian family or the Roman state. That he had been his best soldier, and he often saw him fight against the enemy. Spurius Furius stated that Caeso had come to his aid when he was in danger, sent by Titus Quinctius. He believed that no one else had done more in saving the day.

Lucius Lucretius, the previous year's consul and basking in his own glory, praised Caeso's contributions to his own victories. He recounted their battles and detailed Caeso's notable deeds, both on expeditions and in the field. He urged the plebeians to choose this exceptional young man, blessed with natural talent and high social status, as their fellow citizen rather than drive him to flee Rome and become a citizen of one of Rome's enemies. Any negative aspects of Caeso's character, such as his hot temper, would lessen over time, while his wisdom would grow. As Caeso's flaws decreased and his virtues matured, they should allow such a distinguished man to grow old and live out the remainder of his years in their state.

Among the supporters was his father, Lucius Quinctius Cincinnatus, also known as Cincinnatus. Rather than focusing on his son's merits, which might increase public resentment, he asked for forgiveness for his son's mistakes and youthful indiscretions. He pleaded with them to forgive his youthful son for his sake, as he, Cincinnatus, had never offended anyone with his words or actions. However, some plebeians, out of respect or fear, refused to listen to Cincinnatus' pleas. Others, who felt that they themselves or their friends had been wronged, indicated their verdict with their harsh responses.

A DAMNING CHARGE

13. Over and above the general dislike for Caeso, one accusation against him was particularly damning. Marcus Volscius Fictor, who had been a tribune several years prior, stepped forward as a witness. He claimed that shortly after the plague had hit Rome, he encountered a gang of young men who had been prowling the streets of the Suburra neighborhood. A fight broke out, and his older brother, still recovering from illness, was knocked down and nearly killed by a punch from

Caeso. He was picked up and carried home, and Volscius believed that his brother died from that punch. He also claimed that previous consuls hadn't allowed him to pursue the matter.

As Volscius made these accusations loudly, the men hearing the story became so irritated and outraged that Caeso was almost killed by the mob. Then the tribune, Verginius, ordered him to be arrested and taken to jail. The patricians resisted with force, meeting violence with violence. Titus Quinctius, who had come to his defense earlier, argued that a person who was scheduled for a capital offense trial shouldn't be mistreated before the trial and without a sentence being passed. Verginius responded that he wouldn't punish him before conviction, but he would keep him in jail until the trial date. This would give the Roman people a chance to punish a homicide if found guilty.

The tribunes were appealed to, but they protected their power by taking a middle ground. They prohibited Caeso from being jailed but expressed their desire for the accused to appear at his trial. The tribunes also wanted a sum of money to be promised to the plebeians if Caeso didn't show up. The amount of money to be promised was debated and referred to the Senate. Caeso was held in the public assembly until the patricians could be consulted. It was decided that he should give a surety bond. Each *surety* was set at three-thousand pounds *aes rude, or* bronze nuggets. The number of sureties to be given was left to the tribunes, who set the limit at ten. The prosecutor released the accused for ten sureties, or approximately one-hundred fifty-thousand pounds aes rude. This was the first time that public sureties were provided for a state trial.

After being released from the Forum, Caeso fled from Rome and went into exile among the Etruscans the following night. When it was argued at the trial that he had left his home to go into exile, Tribune Verginius nevertheless still tried to hold the trial, but his colleagues, when appealed to, stopped the trial and dismissed the assembly. The fine was mercilessly enforced on Caeso's father, Cincinnatus, however. After selling all his possessions to pay for it, Cincinnatus lived for a long time in a secluded hut on the other side of the Tiber River, as if in exile.

This trial and the proposal of the Terentillian Law kept the state busy. There was peace from foreign threats, however.

PRIVATE ANGER, PUBLIC RESTRAINT

14. The patricians were silenced by the exile of Caeso, whereas the tribunes, feeling victorious, thought that the Terentillian Law was as good as passed. As far as the older patricians, they had given up their part in governing the state. The younger patricians, especially those close to Caeso, were more bitter than ever against the plebeians, and quite as aggressive. Yet, they promoted their cause by dampening their fury with a kind of moderation.

When the Terentillian Law was first proposed after Caeso's exile, the young patricians were organized and ready. They came prepared with a large army of *clients*, or freed slaves, who attacked the tribunes whenever the tribunes tried to remove them. No single person stood out for praise or blame. The plebeians complained that a thousand Caesos had now replaced the one.

On the days when the tribunes didn't push for the Terentillian Law, though, these same young patricians were calm and peaceful. They greeted the plebeians politely, engaged in conversation, and invited them into their homes. They went to the Forum and let the tribunes hold their meetings without interrupting them. They were never rude to anyone, either in public or private, unless the Terentillian Law was being discussed. So, at all other times, the young patricians were well-liked. As such, the tribunes conducted all their other business without disruption. They were even re-elected for the next year without any offensive remarks or violence. By calming and managing the plebeians, the patricians gradually made them more cooperative. Using these methods, the patricians managed to avoid the Terentillian Law for the entire year.

Chapter 5
EXILE AND SLAVE REBELLION (460 BC)

15. THE NEXT CONSULS, Caius Claudius Sabinus Regillensis, son of Appius Claudius, and Publius Valerius Publicola, [descendant of one of the original consuls, Publius Valerius Publicola], found Rome in a peaceful state. The new year hadn't brought any changes.

Political focus still remained on passing the Terentillian Law or accepting it, and this occupied everyone's mind. The younger senators tried to win the favor of the plebeians, but the tribunes worked even harder to oppose them. The tribunes made the senators look suspicious to the plebeians by claiming that there was a conspiracy, that Caeso was in Rome, and that there were plans to kill the tribunes and the plebeians. The tribunes also claimed that the older patricians had ordered the young men to remove the tribune's power from the state and return the government to its previous form before the occupation of the Sacred Mount.

There was more fear of war from the Volscians and Aequians, which had now become a regular, annual recurrence. It had become such a routine thing that the people developed anxiety from knowing that it would happen every year, like clockwork.

A FIGHT FOR THE MOST MISERABLE OF ALL

Another problem arose, unexpectedly, closer to home. Exiles and slaves, approximately two thousand five hundred men, took over the Capitoline Hill and the Citadel at night. Their leader was Appius Herdonius, a Sabine. Those in the Citadel who didn't want to join the conspirators and take up arms were instantly massacred. Some people, in their panic, ran down to the Forum. The cries of "To arms!" and "The enemy is in the City!" were heard alternately.

The consuls were afraid to arm the plebeians, but they were also afraid to leave them unarmed. The consuls were unsure what sudden disaster had hit Rome, whether it was citizens or foreigners, whether it was due to hatred of plebeians or to betrayal by slaves. The consuls tried to calm the chaos, but by trying to control it, they made it worse. In their frightened and terrified state, the plebeians couldn't be controlled. They eventually distributed weapons, but not to everyone. They wanted to ensure that there was enough protection for all emergencies, even though the enemy was still unknown. The consuls posted guards throughout the City during the night, worried and unsure about who and how many enemies there actually were.

When daylight came, the war and its leader were revealed. Appius Herdonius called from the Capitoline Hill, announcing that this was an opportunity for the slaves to win their freedom. This fight was for the most miserable of all to bring back those who had been wrongfully exiled, and to remove the heavy yokes from necks of the slaves. They would rather do this with the approval of the Roman people; however, if this was a hopeless request, they would take the risky path of stirring up the Volscians and Aequians.

An Enemy in Every House

16. The situation started to become clearer to the patricians and the consuls. However, they feared that this could be a plot by the Veiians or Sabines. With so many enemies in the City, they worried that the Sabine and Etruscan forces might attack as part of a planned strategy. The consuls and patricians also feared that their long-time enemies, the Volscians and Aequians, might not just invade their lands as before, but now attack their City, as it was now already partially captured.

The patricians had many fears, and one of the most significant was the fear of their slaves. They were worried that each house might be harboring an enemy, someone who was neither safe to trust nor safe to distrust, as not trusting them might make them more hostile and determined. Overcoming these kinds of overwhelming dangers could only be done with unity between Rome's classes.

No one feared the tribunes or the plebeians like they feared the slaves. That evil was under control, as it only broke out whenever there was a relief from other evils, and right now it was focused on the fear of foreign aggression. Yet, this issue, more than anything else, helped to depress the fortunes of a sinking State. The tribunes were so irrational and in a frenzy as they argued that the war was fake, a mere illusion created to distract the plebeians from the Terentillian Law. The tribunes claimed that the patricians' friends and clients would leave even quieter than they arrived once they had realized that their noisy efforts to prevent the passing of the Terentillian Law were useless. The tribunes then summoned the people to put their arms aside and hold a council meeting to pass the Terentillian Law.

Meanwhile, the consuls called a meeting of the Senate, revealing themselves to be in greater fear of the tribunes than a nocturnal enemy.

"RESPECT YOUR GODS, IF NOT YOUR CITY"

17. When the news broke that the soldiers were laying down their weapons and leaving their posts, Consul Valerius quickly left the Senate and ran to the tribunes in the comitium. Consul Claudius was left to keep the Senate together.

"What is happening here?" Valerius asked the tribunes. "Are you planning to overthrow the state under the leadership of this rebel leader, Appius Herdonius? Has he managed to corrupt you, even though he couldn't even influence your slaves to join him? Is it when we're under an existential threat by the enemy that you want us to drop all our weapons and rationally discuss laws?"

He turned to the plebeians: "If you don't care about your City or yourselves, at least respect your country's gods [and their temples], which are now held captive by the enemy. Jupiter Optimus Maximus, Juno Regina, Minerva, and the other gods and goddesses are under siege. The enemy's camp now holds the state's protective gods."

"Does this seem sane to you? There are enemies not just within our walls, but barricaded inside our Citadel, overlooking the Forum and Senate. Yet, it's business as usual. Meetings are still being held in the Forum; the Senate is in session, just as if everything were peaceful; the senator gives his opinion, the other Romans cast their votes."

"Shouldn't all patricians and plebeians, consuls, tribunes, gods, and men rush to the Capitoline Hill with weapons in their hands, to free and restore peace to Jupiter Optimus Maximus' sacred home? Oh, Father Romulus! Inspire your descendants with the same determination you had when you reclaimed the Citadel from these same Sabines when they had captured it using gold. Let them follow the same path you and your army took. I, as Consul, will be the first to follow you and your footsteps, as much as a mortal can follow a god."

SEDITION AS A SPECTACLE FOR THE ENEMIES

He ended his speech by saying that he would take up arms, and then call the citizens to their arms. If anyone obstructed him, whether a consul, a tribune, or anyone else, whoever it might be, wherever they might be, on the Capitoline Hill or in the Forum, they would be treated as an enemy. He would ignore the limits to his power as a consul. Should the tribunes order arms to be taken up against Publius Valerius as they had prohibited the taking up arms against Appius Herdonius, he threatened that he would do to the tribunes what the head of his family had dared to do against the kings.

It was evident that Roman sedition was about to erupt in the City and the spectacle would be a delight to the enemy. However, the Terentillian Law couldn't be voted upon, nor would the Consul go to the Capitoline Hill, as nightfall ultimately put an end to the conflict; the tribunes retired, fearing the consuls' weapons. With the instigators of the revolt gone, the patricians then went among the plebeians, joining their conversations and offering advice. The patricians warned the plebeians to be careful of the danger they were putting the state in; that the fight wasn't between the patricians and the plebeians, but that both groups, along with the Citadel, the temples of the gods, and the protective gods of the state and private families, were being surrendered to the enemy.

While these discussions were taking place in the Forum to calm the disturbances, the consuls, in the meantime, had set out around the City gates and walls, in case the Sabines or the Veiians made a move.

Do Not Wait for a Request for Help

18. On the same night, messengers from Rome arrived in Tusculum with news that the Citadel had been captured, the Capitoline Hill seized, and the City was in a state of chaos. At that time, Lucius

Mamilius was the dictator in Tusculum. He quickly called a meeting of the Tusculum senate and introduced the messengers. Mamilius strongly suggested that they shouldn't wait for ambassadors from Rome to come requesting help. The criticality of the situation, their treaties, and even the gods, themselves, called upon them to act. The gods, he said, would never give them a better chance to help earn the gratitude of such a powerful and close neighbor. The senate resolved to send help.

Young Tusculum men were enlisted and issued arms. As the Tusculum allies arrived in Rome at dawn, they were initially thought to be enemies from a distance. It seemed as if the Aequians or Volscians were invading. Once the misunderstanding was cleared up, the Tusculum allies were allowed into the City and they gathered in the Forum where Consul Valerius, who had left Consul Claudius to direct troops guarding the gates, was preparing for battle.

The personal influence of Valerius had won. He assured everyone by saying that when the Capitoline Hill was recovered and peace would be restored to the City, he would like to show everyone what was hidden in the Terentillian Law that the tribunes were trying to pass. He was mindful of his heritage, that the name Publicola, 'the people's friend', carried with it a responsibility of care and that he wouldn't stand in the way of the plebeians' assembly.

Despite the tribunes' efforts to restrain them, Valerius led the troops up the Capitoline Hill where they formed a battle line with the legion from Tusculum alongside them. Both allies and citizens competed for the honor of reclaiming the Citadel. Each leader encouraged his own men. The enemy's morale diminished when they realized they could only rely on their strategic location for protection, and nothing else.

The Romans and allies charged, bursting into the temple's vestibule when Valerius, who was in front, was killed while directing the attack. Publius Volumnius, a former consul, saw him fall. He ordered his men to protect the body and took over the consul's duties. The Roman soldiers were so eager and aggressive that they didn't realize what had happened; they won the battle before they realized they were fighting without a leader. Many of the exiles were cut down, staining the temple with their blood. Others were captured alive. Appius Herdonius, the leader, was killed.

The Capitoline Hill was thus reclaimed, cleansed and purified. The prisoners were punished according to their status, whether they were free or enslaved. A vote of thanks was given from the Senate to the Tusculans for their bravery. It's said that the plebeians threw currency into Consul Valerius' house so that he could be carried out with a more magnificent funeral than he would have had otherwise.

Chapter 6

THE RISE OF CINCINNATUS (460 BC)

19. WHEN ORDER AND peace were restored, the tribunes urged the patricians to fulfill the promise of Consul Valerius. They also urged Consul Claudius to protect his colleague's reputation from any breach of faith and allow the Terentillian Law proceedings to continue. However, the Consul refused to allow the Terentillian Law's discussion to continue until a new colleague replaced the deceased one. These disagreements continued until the elections for a new consul.

In December, due to the patricians' strong efforts, Lucius Quinctius Cincinnatus, Caeso Quinctius' father, was elected consul and would start his duties immediately. The plebeians were worried about having a consul who was angry with them, supported by the patricians, and who had three sons just as spirited as Caeso but with more prudence and moderation.

Upon taking office, Consul Cincinnatus frequently spoke from the tribunal, criticizing both the plebeians and the Senate.

The apathy of the plebeians, he maintained, allowed the tribunes to remain perpetually in office, winning re-election after re-election. These tribunes were acting like kings through their speeches and prosecutions, acting like the heads of a disorganized household and not as people entrusted with the public affairs of the Roman people.

He argued that his son Caeso, a man of courage and constancy, had been driven out of Rome, while these talkative and disruptive men, re-elected tribunes, were ruling with the power of tyrants:

FALSE CLAIMS DESERVE HARSHER PUNISHMENT

"Did the tribune Verginius, simply because he wasn't present on the Capitoline Hill, deserve less punishment than Appius Herdonius, the rebellion leader? No. In fact, he deserved much more punishment if one were to evaluate the situation honestly. Herdonius, to his credit, at least openly declared himself an enemy and, to some extent, incited you all to take up arms. Meanwhile, Verginius, by saying that the war was fake and denying its existence, not only disarmed you but also left you defenseless against your own slaves and exiles."

"And tell me, without disrespect to Consuls Claudius and Valerius, did you march toward the Capitoline Hill before eliminating these threats from the Forum? It's an affront to both gods and men that while these enemies occupied the Citadel and the Capitoline Hill itself, with the leader of the slaves and exiles defiling every sacred space and temple, Rome hesitated to take action. In fact, arms were first raised at Tusculum, not even in Rome!"

"The deliverance of Rome's Citadel hung in the balance, uncertain whether it would come from the Tuscan general, Lucius Mamilius, or from Consuls Valerius and Claudius. We, who deny our Latin allies the right to defend themselves against invasion, would have faced utter destruction if these very same Latins hadn't taken up arms, unprompted, to come save us."

Is This What You Call "Protecting" the People?

"Is this, tribunes, what you call 'protecting' the plebeians? Delivering them up to be ruthlessly slaughtered by the enemy? Even if the lowliest man of your plebeians, which you've isolated from the rest of the plebeians and made into your own province, your own state — even if such a person were to report being attacked by armed slaves and his house stolen, surely you would feel obliged to offer aid. Was Jupiter Optimus Maximus, when his temple was attacked by the armed slaves and exiles, undeserving of any human assistance? These plebeians demand sacred inviolability only for themselves, while even the gods aren't regarded as sacred or inviolable in their eyes."

"But, immersed as you are in crimes against both gods and men, you declare that you'll push your Law through this year. If you do, mark my words, the day of my consulship will be a darker day for this state than the day Publius Valerius was killed. Romans, let it be known that our first action, my colleague's and mine, will be to march the legions against the Volscians and Aequians. By some odd twist of fate, the gods seem more favorable when we're at war than in times of peace."

"What incredible danger we could have been in if those states had known the entire Capitoline Hill was in the hands of exiles and slaves. It's much better to conjecture from the past than to feel it through actual experience."

"We Have No Need For A Draft"

20. Cincinnatus' speech had a significant impact on the plebeians. The patricians, regaining their confidence, saw this as a restoration of the state. Consul Claudius, more enthusiastic in supporting than initi-

ating, allowed his colleague to take the lead. He took on the consular duty of implementing the plan. The tribunes, dismissing these statements as meaningless, questioned how the consuls would mobilize the army when no one would allow them to hold a draft. "But we have no need for a draft," said Cincinnatus, "for when Consul Valerius armed the plebeians to reclaim the Capitoline Hill, they swore an oath to assemble at the consul's command and not to disperse without his order. Therefore, we command that all who took the oath report tomorrow, armed, at Lake Regillus."

The tribunes tried to free the plebeians from their oath, arguing that Cincinnatus was a private citizen when they swore it. However, the disregard for the gods that is common today hadn't yet taken hold. Plebeians didn't twist oaths and laws to suit their needs, but instead adjusted their behavior to comply with them. The tribunes, seeing no way to stop the mobilization, tried to delay it.

Rumors had spread that the augurs were to meet at Lake Regillus to consecrate a place where the auspices could be taken, and plebeians could conduct business under favorable omens. Any laws passed in Rome by the tribunes would have no effect there. Everyone would vote as the consuls wished, as there was no right to appeal more than a mile from the City. The tribunes would be subject to the consuls' authority if they went there. These rumors worried the tribunes, but what scared them most was Cincinnatus' repeated statement that he wouldn't hold an election for consuls. He believed the state was so sick that ordinary remedies couldn't cure it. The republic needed a dictator, so that anyone who disturbed the peace would face a dictatorship, without the right to appeal.

REAPPOINTING THE SAME PEOPLE ISN'T WORK-ING

21. The Senate was gathering on the Capitoline Hill as tribunes arrived with the agitated plebeians. The crowd, screaming loudly, sought protection of the consuls and then the senators. However, they couldn't persuade the Consul to change his mind until the tribunes agreed to follow the authority of the Senate. Cincinnatus presented the tribunes' and the plebeians' demands. The Senate passed resolutions that the tribunes shouldn't propose the Terentillian Law that year, and the consuls shouldn't lead the army out of the City.

The Senate also decided to keep the same magistrates and continue reappointing the same tribunes. Anything else, they believed, would be detrimental to the republic. The consuls obeyed the Senate's authority; however, the same tribunes were appointed again despite the consuls' objections. The patricians, not wanting to give in to the plebeians, re-elected Lucius Quinctius Cincinnatus as consul. This was the most heated issue of the year.

"Should I be surprised," Cincinnatus said to the senators, "that your authority carries little weight, senators? You, yourselves, are undermining it. Since the plebeians have ignored your Senate decree regarding successive terms, you also want to ignore it because you don't want to appear weaker than the plebeians. As if having more power in the state means being more inconsistent and more unruly! It's certainly more inconsistent and foolish to disregard one's own decrees and resolutions than those of others."

"Follow the thoughtless crowd, senators, and you, who should be setting an example, are breaking the rules because of others' actions, rather than having others follow your good example. I won't follow the tribunes or allow myself to be re-elected consul against a Senate

decree. I advise you, Consul Claudius, to control the Roman plebeians' recklessness. Understand that I won't consider your actions
as an obstacle to my honor. Instead, the glory from me declining the
honor is increased and the hatred that people would feel if we allow
this to continue is decreased."

They then jointly issued this order: No one should try to make
Cincinnatus consul. If anyone did, they wouldn't accept that vote.

Chapter 7

ESCALATION WITH VOLSCIANS AND AEQUIANS (459-458 BC)

22. QUINTUS FABIUS VIBULANUS was elected consul for the third time, along with Lucius Cornelius Maluginensis.

That year, the census was conducted. However, the lustrum purification sacrifice wasn't performed because of scruples about how the Capitoline Hill had been seized and how the former consul had been slain.

The consulship of Quintus Fabius and Lucius Cornelius was a difficult one from the very beginning of the year. Conflicts erupted as the tribunes began to instigate the plebeians. Latins and Hernician allies reported that the Volscians and Aequians were preparing for a large-scale war. Volscian troops were already in Antium. There was also a fear that the colony itself might rebel. The tribunes reluctantly agreed to prioritize the war.

A LARGE-SCALE WAR

The consuls divided the responsibilities. Consul Fabius was tasked with leading the legions to Antium, while Consul Cornelius was to defend the City from any enemy attacks. The Hernician and Latin allies were ordered to provide soldiers, as per their treaty. The army was composed of two-thirds allies and one-third Roman citizens.

When the allies arrived on the appointed day, Consul Fabius set up his camp outside the Capuan Gate. After performing a purification rite for the army, he marched toward Antium and halted at a short distance from the city and the Volscians' camp. As the Aequians hadn't yet arrived, the Volscians were unwilling to engage in battle. Instead, the Volscians prepared to defend themselves within their fortifications. The next day, the Consul separated out the Romans, Hernicians and Latins into three separate groups, one from each nation, around the enemy's fortifications. He would be in the middle with the Roman legions. The Consul instructed them to observe his signals carefully so that each division could both start and stop the battle together. He then positioned cavalry behind each respective division.

Using this formation, Consul Fabius then charged the camp, immediately dislodging the Volscians from their entrenchments, as they were unable to protect themselves from all sides simultaneously. Fabius got inside the Volscian lines and drove the panic-stricken mob, now moving in a single direction, out of their camp. The cavalry had been mere spectators of the fight until then, as the horses couldn't enter the fortifications. With the soldiers fleeing in disarray onto the open plain, the cavalry now intercepted the Volscians and shared in the victory by cutting down the terrified troops. The slaughter of the fleeing troops was great, both in the camp and outside the lines, but the spoils of war were even greater because the enemy could barely carry their weapons with them as they ran.

The entire Volscian army would have been destroyed if the forest hadn't provided them cover during their flight.

REPAYING TUSCULUM'S KINDNESS

23. While these events were happening in Antium, the Aequians sent their strongest young men to attack and capture the Tusculum citadel at night. The rest of the Aequian army halted and set up camp not far from Tusculum's walls in order to distract the enemy. When news of this reached Rome and then Antium, the Romans were as shocked as if they had heard their own Capitoline Hill had been taken.

The Tusculans had recently helped them, and the similar danger they now faced seemed to demand a return of that aid. Consul Fabius quickly moved all the goods they had taken from the Volscians' camp to Antium. He left a small group of soldiers to guard Antium, then rushed the rest of his army to Tusculum. The soldiers were only allowed to bring their weapons and any baked bread that was at hand. Consul Cornelius sent more supplies from Rome.

The ensuing war in Tusculum went on for several months. With one part of the army laying siege to the Aequian camp, Consul Fabius lent another part of the army to the Tusculans to help them take back their citadel. The Tusculans couldn't have done it by direct assault. After being brought to the point of total desperation, the Aequians were forced to leave the citadel because they were starving. The Tusculans made the Aequians walk under a yoke, unarmed and naked, as a sign of defeat. As the Aequians shamefully fled home, they were overtaken by Consul Fabius on Mount Algidus and were all killed, leaving no survivors.

After this victory, Consul Fabius moved his army back to Columen and set up camp. Consul Cornelius left Rome once the City was no longer in danger. The two consuls then entered enemy territory from different directions and each tried to outdo the other in damage: Volscians on the one side and the Aequians on the other.

Some historians say that the people of Antium rebelled that same year. They claim that Consul Cornelius led the war and recaptured the town. However, I can't confirm this because the older records don't mention it.

A BULLY WAS BULLIED?

24. Immediately after the war had ended, a political conflict within the City caused concern for the Senate. The tribunes claimed that the army was kept abroad dishonestly, under false pretenses, with the intention of frustrating the passage of the Terentillian Law. Regardless, the tribunes vowed to continue their efforts. Publius Lucretius, the City's prefect, managed to delay the tribunes' actions until the consuls returned.

Another issue emerged when Aulus Cornelius and Quintus Servilius, the *quaestors*, set a trial date for Marcus Volscius. He was accused of providing false testimony against Caeso Quinctius. Evidence showed that Volscius' brother, who was supposedly attacked by Caeso, had been bedridden due to a long-term illness. He hadn't been seen in public and died from the illness a month after the incident. Furthermore, Caeso wasn't in Rome at the time of the alleged crime, as confirmed by his fellow soldiers who stated that he was quartered with them and hadn't had a leave of absence. To prove his accusations, many privately supported the idea of bringing Volscius to a private judge. Since he dared not go to trial, all the issues converging in one made the conviction of Volscius as certain as if Caeso had testified against him.

The tribunes delayed the proceedings against Volscius, insisting that the Terentillian Law must be addressed before the trial could proceed. This resulted in both issues being postponed until the consuls' return. When the consuls returned victorious, many believed the tribunes were intimidated into silence about the Terentillian Law. However, the tribunes were instead focused on securing a fourth term and shifted their efforts toward the election. Despite the consuls' efforts, the tribunes won the election.

That same year, peace was granted to the Aequians.

The census, which had begun the previous year, was completed, and the lustrum purification ritual was then performed. It was said to have been the tenth lustrum since the beginning of the City. The numbers from the census amounted to one hundred seventeen thousand three hundred nineteen citizens.

Praised for their achievements both in war and at home, the consuls managed to maintain peace both domestically and abroad. Despite some discord, the state was less troubled than in previous times.

458 BC — THE AEQUIANS BREAK THE TREATY

25. Lucius Minucius Esquilinus Augurinus and Caius Nautius Rutilus were elected as the next consuls.

The consuls inherited two unresolved issues from the previous year. As was before, the consuls were against the Terentillian Law, while the tribunes opposed the trial of Volscius. However, the new quaestors held more power and influence.

Marcus Valerius, son of previous consul Publius Valerius and grandson of Volesus Valerius, was appointed quaestor alongside Titus Quinctius Capitolinus, who had been consul three times. Quaestor Quinctius couldn't restore Caeso Quinctius and return him to the Quinctian family or to Rome. Instead, he waged war on Volscius in order to bring him to justice for being a false witness who had stripped an innocent man of the right to defend himself.

Tribune Verginius was the most active in pushing for the Terentillian Law to be passed. The consuls were given two months to investigate the measure and inform the plebeians about any hidden intentions behind it. The consuls would then allow them to vote. This delay brought peace to the City.

However, the Aequians didn't let them rest for long.

The Aequians broke the treaty they had made with the Romans the previous year and appointed Cloelius Gracchus as their chief commander, a prominent figure among the Aequians. Under Gracchus' command, the Aequians attacked the district of Labicum, then Tusculum, and set up their camp at Algidum with their stolen goods.

TELL IT TO THE OAK TREE

Former consuls Quintus Fabius, Publius Volumnius, and Aulus Posthumius served as envoys, going to the Aequian camp to protest the attacks and demand restitution according to the treaty. General Gracchus' quarters were located under a large shady oak tree.

Gracchus told the Roman envoys to recite their message from the Roman Senate to the oak tree while he attended to other, more important matters. Accordingly, the envoys began leaving when one of the envoys shouted, "May this sacred oak and all the gods hear how you have broken the treaty! May the gods support our complaints now and our weapons later when we avenge the rights of gods and men that you have violated!"

When the envoys returned to Rome, the Senate ordered one of the consuls to march his army against General Gracchus at Algidum. The other consul was tasked with destroying the Aequians' land. The tribunes tried to stop the recruitment of soldiers, and they might have succeeded if not for a sudden new threat.

Chapter 8

Cincinnatus Becomes Dictator (458 BC)

26. A LARGE HORDE of Sabines came very close to the walls of the City, having laid waste to the fields and terrifying the citizens along the way. The plebeians willingly took up arms and two large armies were formed, despite the tribunes' protests.

Consul Nautius led one of these armies against the Sabines. He set up his entrenched camp at Eretum, chiefly using small expeditions to carry out night raids. Nautius repaid such incredible devastation to the Sabine territory that the Roman lands seemed almost untouched by the enemy in comparison.

However, Consul Minucius didn't have the same success or determination with his army. He ordered camp set up not far from the enemy and, out of fear, he stayed within the camp. When the enemy noticed this, they became more audacious, as sometimes happens when an opponent shows fear, and they attacked his camp at night. When that didn't work, the Sabines surrounded the Roman camp the next day. Before the Sabines could completely block all the exits, five horsemen managed to get through the enemy lines and brought the news to Rome that Consul Minucius and his army were blockaded inside their camp.

This was completely unexpected and caused great panic and alarm, as if the City, not just the camp, was under siege. The Senate called for Consul Nautius, but when he was unable to provide enough protection, they decided to appoint a dictator to manage the situation.

By universal consent, Lucius Quinctius Cincinnatus was chosen as the right one to be dictator.

FROM FARMER TO DICTATOR

This story is worth hearing for those who scorn everything human in favor of wealth, who think there is no place for great honor or virtue unless riches overflow in abundance. The last hope of Rome, Lucius Quinctius Cincinnatus, was now spending his remaining days tending a modest four-acre field across the Tiber River, opposite the present-day shipyards, known as the Quinctian Meadows. There he was found by a delegation from the Senate, who approached him as he was either digging out a ditch or plowing, focused on his work.

After mutual greetings, the delegation asked him to put on his toga so that he could hear the Senate's mandate, and expressed hope that it might turn out well for him and for the City. Cincinnatus asked them, still utterly surprised, "Is all well?" and asked his wife, Racilia, to run and get his toga quickly from the cottage. After wiping off the dust and perspiration, Cincinnatus put on his toga. As he came forward to join the delegation, they saluted him as dictator and congratulated him, summoning him to the City and explaining the urgent situation with the army.

The government had arranged a boat for him to leave at once. Upon crossing the river, he was welcomed by his three sons, other relatives, friends, and a significant portion of the Senate. He was then escorted by a large crowd and preceded by lictors, to his residence. There was also a sizable gathering of plebeians who weren't too happy to see Cincinnatus. Many viewed his newfound authority as excessive and saw him as a potentially dangerous figure.

That night, the main focus was on ensuring the City's security. No major actions were taken beyond strengthening the guard.

"STANDARD-BEARER, MOVE FASTER!"

27. The following day, Dictator Cincinnatus arrived in the Forum before dawn. He appointed Lucius Tarquitius as his lieutenant, his *Master of the Horse [Magister Equitum]*. Tarquitius was a man from a noble family, but one who had been a foot-soldier because of poverty. Despite his limited resources, Tarquitius was widely regarded as the most skilled military strategist among Rome's young men.

The Dictator, accompanied by his Master of the Horse, proceeded to the assembly and announced a halt to all civil activities. He ordered all shops in the City to close and prohibited anyone from transacting any private business whatsoever. He then instructed all men of military age to gather in the Campus Martius before sunset, armed and carrying provisions for five days plus twelve stakes to make a *palisade*, a fence fortification.

He also ordered those too old for military service to prepare food for the army while the soldiers prepared their weapons and gathered the stakes. The young men scattered in various directions to find stakes, taking them from the nearest places they could find. No one was hindered and everyone complied with the Dictator's orders promptly.

The troops were now assembled, ready to march and, if necessary, battle. Dictator Cincinnatus led the legions, with the Master of the Horse leading the cavalry. Both groups were given encouragement suitable to the emergency: they needed to march faster than usual to reach the enemy by nightfall. Consul Minucius and the Roman soldiers were under siege and had been blockaded now for three days. The outcome of this critical situation could change at any moment. To show their commitment, the soldiers shouted out to each other, "Standard-bearer, move faster! Follow, soldiers!"

Cincinnatus' army arrived at Algidum at midnight and, as soon as Dictator Cincinnatus realized they were within striking distance of the enemy, they halted.

THE CIRCUMVALLATION STRATEGY

28. After riding around and surveying the enemy camp to understand its layout as much as possible in the darkness, the Dictator ordered the military tribunes to instruct the soldiers to throw down their packs in one place and then return back to their positions with their weapons and stakes. The orders were carried out promptly. Then, maintaining the discipline the soldiers had shown during their march, he arranged the entire army in a long column surrounding enemy lines. He instructed them that, at a given signal, the troops should all shout, and, after shouting, every man should dig a trench in front of his own position and use his stakes to erect a palisade. Shortly after issuing these orders, the signal was given. The soldiers did as they were told and began building, their shouts echoing around the enemy blockade and reaching Consul Minucius' camp.

In the enemy camp, there was immediate panic, however, in the Romans' camp they began to rejoice, excitedly reassuring each other that help was on the way. The Romans began to intimidate the enemy from their watch posts, using sorties to harass them. Consul Minucius declared that there was no time to waste. He believed that the shout not only signaled the arrival of their allies, but that he would be surprised if the enemy camp wasn't already under attack from the outside. Minucius ordered his men to arm themselves and follow him immediately.

Consul Minucius began the battle at night, signaling to Cincinnatus with a shout that they were also beginning their fight, as well. As the Aequians were busy trying to stop the *circumvallation* around them by Cincinnatus' army, Consul Minucius' army burst out of their camp and started to battle. The Aequians, taken by surprise, then shifted their focus from the Romans on the outer fortifications back to the Romans inside the camp. In this way, Minucius' constant distractions allowed the work on the outer fortifications to continue, uninterrupted, throughout the night. The Aequians were kept occupied by Consul Minucius until dawn.

At daybreak, the Aequians found themselves surrounded by the Dictator's fortifications on one side and were barely able to hold off Minucius' army on the other side. Cincinnatus' army, having completed their work, returned to their weapons and then moved in. The Aequians were now facing danger from two sides, and neither side was letting up.

Under the stress of being attacked on both sides, the Aequians stopped fighting and resorted to pleading with the Dictator and the Consul, begging them to please not make the price of victory to be their extermination. Instead, they asked, please allow them to surrender their weapons and leave. Consul Minucius referred the matter to Dictator Cincinnatus.

Cincinnatus was furious. In his anger, he was determined to humiliate them. He ordered that Cloelius Gracchus, their general, and other high-ranking leaders, be brought to him in chains. The town of Corbio would be evacuated. The Dictator said he didn't want the blood of the Aequians, but rather a confession from them that they had been defeated and subdued. He ordered them to pass under the yoke, a symbol of submission made of three spears, two planted in the ground and one tied across the top. The Dictator sent the Aequians under this yoke and allowed them to depart.

TRIUMPH

29. The Aequian camp was found to be stocked full of supplies left behind (as he had sent the Aequians away naked). Cincinnatus distributed all the spoils to his own soldiers, since they had been ordered to leave Rome so quickly and with very little.

He criticized Consul Minucius' army and the consul himself, saying, "Soldiers, you won't receive any part of the spoils taken from the enemy who nearly defeated you. And you, Lucius Minucius, until you show the spirit of a consul, you'll command these legions as a lieutenant." Minucius resigned his position as consul and stayed with the army, as ordered.

Plebeians at that time were very obedient to authority, especially when it was combined with superior merit. The army, remembering Dictator Cincinnatus' kindness more than his criticisms, awarded him a golden crown and hailed him as their protector.

The Senate, convened by former consul Quintus Fabius, decreed that Cincinnatus should enter Rome in a triumphant procession with his troops that accompanied him. The defeated Aequian leaders were paraded before his chariot, the military standards were carried on ahead, and after that his army followed, laden with spoils. It's said that tables with food were set out in front of all the houses, and the soldiers, feasting as they marched, followed the chariot, singing songs of victory and making jokes.

On that day, Lucius Mamilius of Tusculum, who had raised an army to rescue the embattled Romans several years earlier when the Capitoline Hill was taken, was granted citizenship, to universal approval. [This was the first recorded granting of citizenship for service to Rome.]

Dictator Cincinnatus would have resigned his position, but he was kept in office for the trial of Marcus Volscius, [who had lied about Caeso Quinctius]. In awe of Cincinnatus, the tribunes didn't interfere this time. Volscius was found guilty and exiled to Lanuvium.

THE DICTATOR RESIGNS

Cincinnatus resigned his position on the sixteenth day, after holding it for six months.

During this time, Consul Nautius fought the Sabines at Eretum with great success. So, in addition to the destruction of their lands, the Sabines suffered another blow.

Former consul Quintus Fabius was sent to Algidum to replace Lucius Minucius.

Toward the end of the year, the tribunes began to discuss the Terentillian Law, but because two armies were abroad, the patricians decided that no business should be proposed to the plebeians. The plebeians managed to elect the same tribunes for the fifth time.

It's reported that wolves seen on the Capitoline Hill were chased away by dogs, and because of this omen, the Capitoline Hill was purified.

These were the events of that year.

Chapter 9

STUDYING DEMOCRACY (457–452 BC)

30. QUINTUS MINUCIUS ESQUILINUS and Marcus Horatius Pulvillus were the next consuls.

At the start of their term, there was peace outside of Rome. However, inside the City, the same tribunes and the same Terentillian Law were causing unrest. The situation could have escalated further due to high tensions, but news arrived that Aequians had attacked and wiped out the garrison at Corbio. The consuls called a meeting of the Senate and were instructed to quickly draft an army and head to Mount Algidus.

OVEREXTENDED TRIBUNES CALL FOR MORE

The argument about the Terentillian Law was put aside, but a new disagreement arose about the recruitment of the army. The consuls' authority was nearly overpowered with the help of the tribunes when more alarming news arrived: the Sabine army had invaded. They had pillaged Roman territory and were now headed toward Rome.

This was such shocking news that the tribunes allowed the recruitment to proceed, however, they made a condition: since they had been frustrated for the past five years trying to pass the Terentillian Law, the existing tribunate provided little protection for the plebeians; ten tribunes should be elected in the future. The patricians reluctantly agreed to this but insisted that the same tribunes shouldn't be re-elected. An election for the tribunes was held immediately to prevent any further delays after the war. Thirty-six years after the first tribunes, ten were elected, two from each class, and it was decided that future elections would follow this pattern.

The draft was held. Once the army was assembled, Minucius set out against the Sabines. However, he found no enemy. Consul Horatius, after the Aequians had killed the garrison at Corbio and also had taken a garrison at Ortona, fought a battle at Algidum. He killed many enemies and drove them not only from Algidum, but also from Corbio and Ortona. He destroyed Corbio as punishment for the murder of the Roman garrison.

456 BC — PEACEFUL BUT HUNGRY

31. Marcus Valerius Maximus Lactuca and Spurius Verginius Tricostus were elected as the next consuls.

There was peace both domestically and internationally. However, they faced a shortage of food due to heavy rainfall.

A proposal was made to turn the Aventine Hill into public property.

455 BC — TERENTILLIAN LAW SCRAPPED

The same tribunes were re-elected the following year, with Titus Romilius Rocus Vaticanus and Caius Veturius Cicurinus as consuls.

The tribunes strongly advocated for a Terentillian Law in all their speeches. Privately, they were ashamed that, even though their numbers had been increased, the issue remained as neglected during their own term as it had been throughout the previous five years.

While the City was busy with these matters, they received alarming news from Tusculum reporting that the Aequians had invaded the Tusculan territory. People were ashamed, as Tusculum had helped Rome, that there was any delay in providing immediate assistance. Both consuls were dispatched with an army and found the enemy in their usual position in Algidum. A battle ensued, resulting in the death of over seven thousand enemies. The rest were driven away.

The Roman army obtained a large number of spoils, which the consuls sold off due to the treasury's depleted state. This decision was unpopular with the army and it gave the tribunes a reason to impeach the consuls before the plebeians.

454 BC — A SOFTER APPROACH PROMPTS STUDY OF SOLON

As soon as the consuls left office, they were succeeded by Spurius Tarpeius Montanus Capitolinus and Aulus Aternius Varus Fontinalis.

Both prior consuls were immediately impeached upon leaving office. A day for court was set for Titus Romilius by Caius Claudius Cicero, a tribune, and for Caius Veturius by Lucius Alienus, a plebeian aedile. Both were found guilty, to the intense indignation of the patricians. Romilius was fined ten thousand pounds aes rude, and Veturius was fined fifteen thousand pounds aes rude.

The new consuls didn't let the misfortune of their predecessors deter them. They, too, could be condemned, they said, but the plebeians and tribunes wouldn't pass a Terentillian Law. As the enthusiasm for the proposed law died down, having been placed before the people many times, the tribunes chose to abandon it. Instead, they adopted a softer approach with the patricians, suggesting that they should finally resolve their disputes.

If the patricians were displeased with plebeian laws, the tribunes proposed, they should at least allow equal representation; both the plebeians and the patricians should work together to frame laws beneficial to both parties. The patricians didn't reject this proposal in principle, but they insisted that only patricians should propose laws. As they agreed on the most aspects about the law but disagreed on who should propose them, Roman ambassadors were sent to Athens. Spurius Posthumius Albus, Aulus Manlius, and Publius Sulpicius Camerinus were ordered to copy the famous laws of *Solon* and learn about the institutions, customs, and laws of other Greek cities.

32. Overall, the year was peaceful and free from foreign conflicts.

453 BC — FAMINE AND DISEASE

The next year was even more tranquil. Publius Curiatius Fistus Trigeminus and Sextus Quintilius served as consuls.

The tribunes remained quiet, primarily due to their anticipation of the ambassadors' return from Athens and the introduction of foreign laws from what the ambassadors had learned.

Two severe disasters struck simultaneously: famine and disease, both of which were devastating to humans and livestock alike. The lands were abandoned, and the City was drained by a continuous series of deaths. Numerous prominent families were in mourning.

Servilius Cornelius, the Flamen Quirinalis (or high priest), and Caius Horatius Pulvillus, the augur, both passed away. The augurs quickly elected Caius Veturius to replace Pulvillus, particularly because he had been condemned by the plebeians.

Consul Quintilius and four tribunes also died. These multiple tragedies made the year a sorrowful one, but there was complete peace from enemies.

452 BC — THE AMBASSADORS RETURN

Caius (Titus) Menenius Lanatus and Publius Sestius Capitolinus Vaticanus were then elected as consuls.

There were no foreign wars that year, but domestic disturbances emerged. The ambassadors returned with the laws of Athens, and the tribunes insisted that the process of compiling the laws should finally begin.

It was decided that ten men, known as *decemvirs*, would be elected to lead. Under decemvirs, there would be no right to appeal. They would be the only magistrates for that year.

There was a lengthy debate about whether plebeians should be included among them. Eventually, the patricians conceded this was acceptable as long as the Icilian Law regarding compensation to the patricians for lost buildings on the Aventine Hill [the land was being given to the plebeians] and other sacred laws weren't revoked.

Chapter 10
THE DECEMVIRS
(451-450 BC)

33. THREE-HUNDRED AND TWO years after the founding of Rome, the government underwent its second major change. The highest authority shifted from two consuls to a group of ten officials known as *decemvirs*.

This change was similar to the previous transition from kings to consuls. However, it was less significant this time because it didn't last long. The initial excitement of a new government quickly turned into excessive luxury, which then lead to its downfall. At that point, the government returned back to the previous system, where two consuls held the highest authority.

A NEW FORM OF GOVERNMENT

The ten decemvirs appointed were Appius Claudius, Titus Genucius, Publius Sestius, Lucius Veturius, Caius Julius, Aulus Manlius, Publius Sulpicius, Publius Curiatius, Titus Romilius, and Spurius Postumius.

As Appius Claudius and Titus Genucius had been elected to serve as consuls, they were given the honor of being a decemvir as compensation. Publius Sestius, a consul from the previous year, was also included because he had originally proposed this change to the Senate against his colleague's wishes. Three of the decemvirs were from the ambassadors who had traveled to Athens. Their knowledge of foreign laws was considered useful for creating a set of new laws. The remaining four members to complete the group were chosen from older individuals, as they were less likely to strongly oppose the views of others. Appius Claudius was given overall control of the government due to his popularity among the plebeians. He had transformed from being a harsh critic of the plebeians to being their protector and advocate.

The decemvirs rotated daily, each serving justice to the plebeians every tenth day. On these days, the decemvir who acted as chief justice was accompanied by twelve lictors, while his nine colleagues had one lictor each.

Despite their unanimous decisions, which could sometimes be harmful to the governed, the decemvirs showed the utmost fairness to others. For example, even though the decemvirs were appointed without the right to appeal their judgment, when a dead body was dug up in the house of Publius Sestius, a decemvir and a patrician, he was brought before the assembly as the man's guilt was just as clear as the crime was horrific. Caius Julius, one of the decemvirs, set a trial date for Sestius. Julius acted as the prosecutor, even though he had the right to act as sole judge. Instead, he surrendered as judge, thereby placing his power back in the hands of the people.

LAWS OF TEN TABLES

34. Both the highest and lowest in society experienced fair and prompt justice from the decemvirs, as if it were delivered by an oracle. They focused on creating laws, which were eventually inscribed on ten tables and presented in a special assembly for this purpose.

After a special prayer, the decemvirs told everyone to read the proposed laws, intended to benefit the state, the people, and their future generations. Called the Laws of Ten Tables, they were designed to ensure equal rights for all citizens, regardless of their social status. The decemvirs felt that the benefit would be the combined wisdom and abilities of many men. They encouraged everyone to think about each law, discuss it amongst themselves, and bring any perceived excesses or deficiencies to public debate. The goal was to create laws that the plebeians wouldn't only approve, but also feel as if they had proposed, themselves.

Once the laws were adjusted according to public opinion, the Laws of Ten Tables were passed by the Assembly of Centuries. Even in the mass of legislation today, where laws are piled one upon another in a confused heap, the Laws of Ten Tables remain the foundation of all public and private law.

It was generally said that two tables were still needed, and their addition would complete the entire body of Roman law. As the election day approached, this expectation to add the missing tables led to a desire to appoint the decemvirs again. The plebeians, who now disliked the title of "consul" as much as they disliked the title of "king", felt they didn't need the help of the tribunes, as the decemvirs allowed appeals from one to another.

A NEW ELECTION, A NEW APPIUS CLAUDIUS

35. When it was announced that election for the decemvirs for the second time would be in twenty-four days, a strong desire for power emerged. The most influential men in the state began to campaign for the position, humbly asking for the support of the same plebeians they had often clashed with. I think these men feared that if they didn't fill these powerful posts, they would be filled by men who weren't worthy of them.

The risk of losing his position, despite his past honors and age, motivated Appius Claudius, as one of the decemvirs, to begin acting more like someone campaigning for the role than someone who already held it. It was hard to tell if he was a decemvir or a candidate. Claudius criticized the patricians and praised every minor and humble plebeian candidate. He was often seen in the Forum in the company of former tribunes like Duillius and Icilius and used their influence to gain the support of the plebeians.

Claudius' own colleagues, who had previously been loyal to him, started to question his intentions. His sudden friendliness and humility appeared so disingenuous that they suspected that he wasn't preparing to leave office but, instead, looking for ways to stay in power.

The Humility Stratagem

Unable to openly oppose him, however, they decided to humor him by letting him preside over the elections, as he was the youngest. This was a trick which they thought would prevent Appius Claudius from appointing himself, a move that had never been done, except by the tribunes – and even then, only as a very bad precedent.

However, Appius Claudius, assuring all that he would conduct the elections properly, saw this as an opportunity and used it to his advantage. By forming an alliance, he managed, through the election process, to secure the rejection of the two Quinctii — Capitolinus and Cincinnatus — and his own uncle, Caius Claudius, who was one of the staunchest supporters of the patricians, as well as other citizens of high rank. He then helped elect decemvirs who were very far from being equals either socially or politically, with himself at the top. This was a move that was heavily criticized by honorable men, who didn't think he would have the audacity to do it.

With him were elected, from the patricians, Marcus Cornelius Maluginensis, Marcus Sergius Esquilinus, Lucius Minucius Esquilinus, and Quintus Fabius Vibulanus, and, from the plebeians, Quintus Poetelius, Titus Antonius Merenda, Caeso Duillius Longus, Spurius Oppius Cornicen, and Manius Rabuleius.

450 BC — 120 FASCES; AXE OPTIONAL

36. This marked the end of Appius Claudius pretending to be someone he wasn't. From this point forward, he started to live according to his true nature and began to mold his new colleagues before they took office.

The newly elected men had private meetings, daily, away from prying eyes. Then, equipped with their plans for tyranny, which they developed in absolute secrecy, they stopped hiding their arrogance about it. They made themselves hard to get access to. Those who did get access to them were given an unfriendly and stern reception. They continued this way until the fifteenth of May, which was the traditional time for the magistrates to start their office.

At the beginning of their term, the new decemvirs made the first day memorable by creating a scene of great fear. The previous decemvirs had followed the rule that the one person who was in charge that day would have twelve lictors with *fasces,* [the bundle of wooden rods. sometimes with an axe, denoting authority]. Instead, now every decemvir had his own twelve lictors and his own fasces. A total of one-hundred and twenty lictors filled the Forum. The decemvirs explained that it didn't matter if the axe blades were removed or not; they had been appointed with absolute power over life and death, without the right to appeal.

Ten Kings, Zero Accountability

To the people, however, it looked like there were ten kings now. Fear spread not only among the plebeians but also among the leading patricians. They suspected a pretext for bloodshed was being sought. If anyone spoke in favor of freedom, either in the Senate or at a public meeting, the fasces would immediately be brought out to intimidate them.

In addition to the plebeians having no protection now that the right to appeal was abolished, the decemvirs had also agreed not to interfere with each other's sentencing. The previous decemvirs had allowed their legal decisions to be appealed to a colleague and had referred some matters to the plebeians which seemed to fall within their jurisdiction.

For a while, the fear terrorized all classes equally. Gradually, it began to focus solely on the plebeians. The patricians were left alone, while the lower classes were subjected to arbitrary and cruel treatment. The people were judged based on who they were, not the merits of their case. Judgments were made in private and then announced in the Forum. If a plebeian appealed to a decemvir's colleague, they were left in such a state that they *wished* they had accepted the original sentence.

There was also a rumor, without any proof, that the decemvirs had conspired to maintain their tyranny not just for the present, but for the future as well. It was said that the decemvirs had secretly sworn an oath not to hold elections and to keep the decemvirs in power indefinitely.

Young Patricians Turn Violent

37. The plebeians started to observe the faces of the patricians closely. They hoped to gain an understanding about the threat of slavery that had led the republic to its current state. The influential members of the Senate now despised both the decemvirs as well as the plebeians. They didn't agree with what was going on but believed that the plebeians deserved what they received. The patricians didn't want to help those who, in their rush for freedom, had ended up enslaving themselves. They even added to the plebeians' troubles, hoping that the current situation would make them long for the return of two consuls and the old form of government.

Most of the year had passed, and two more sets of laws had been added to the ten sets from the previous year. If these additional laws were also approved in a meeting of the Centuries, the *Comitia Centuriata*, there would be no need for the decemvirs to continue.

The patricians were eagerly waiting to see when the meeting to elect consuls would be announced. The plebeians were trying to figure out how to bring back the power of the tribunes, their protection against the patricians, which had been absent for a long time.

As time passed, no mention was made of the elections.

The decemvirs, who had initially presented themselves to the plebeians while surrounded by ex-tribunes, now protected themselves by gathering young patricians. This band of young patricians crowded the courts, blocked the tribunes, bullied the plebeians, and took their possessions just because they could. These young patricians didn't even spare physical punishment. Some plebeians were beaten with rods, others were beheaded, and the property of the victim was given away to the killer.

Corrupted by such rewards, the young patricians not only didn't resist the lawlessness of the decemvirs, but openly stated that they preferred their own satisfaction over the freedom of all.

Chapter 11
ENEMIES DETECT WEAKNESS (449 BC)

38. THE IDES OF May arrived, and the decemvirs' term of office expired. However, no new election of officials had occurred. The decemvirs were now considered ordinary citizens but they continued as decemvirs, continuing to assert their authority and flaunting the symbols of power. It seemed like a form of royal oppression.

Freedom was mourned as if it were gone forever, with no one stepping up to fight for it. This despair wasn't only felt by the citizens themselves, but also by neighboring states who looked down upon them, outraged that power could exist where freedom was lost.

The Sabines, with a large army, invaded Roman territory and caused widespread destruction, taking away both men and livestock as spoils. They then withdrew the army, which had ranged far and wide, to Eretum. There they set up camp, hoping that the lack of harmony in Rome would stop the draft and prevent the formation of a Roman army.

Not only did the news spread of this invasion, but the flight of the country people into and through the city also caused panic. The decemvirs, with no support from either patrician or plebeian, were uncertain about what to do.

The plebeians and patricians were further alarmed by another disaster. The Aequians, from the opposite side, set up camp at Algidum, and from there were making incursions into the Tusculan territory.

Ambassadors from Tusculum came asking for help from Rome, reporting that their land was being ravaged.

ALONE IN THE SENATE-HOUSE

The panic was so severe that the decemvirs decided to consult the Senate about the City's defenses. Rome was now caught between two wars at the same time. They ordered the senators to the senate-house, knowing they would face a wave of anger and expecting to be blamed for the destruction of the land and other impending dangers. They also understood that there would be attempts to end their rule unless they resisted unanimously and actively suppressed any aggressive attempts using force, if necessary.

When the voice of the herald announced in the Forum that the Senators were to meet before the decemvirs, it caught the attention of the plebeians. They were surprised, as the decemvirs had long since neglected the customary consultation of the Senate. Why, after such a long time, were the decemvirs resuming a forgotten practice? The plebeians, for once, were grateful to both the enemy and their wars for bringing back some semblance of their former free state. The people searched for a senator in the Forum but found few.

The plebeians then noticed the senate-house. The decemvirs were the only ones inside, and they were alone. Were the senators not answering the call to assemble because they were rejecting the decemvirs' rule? The decemvirs believed so. Their government, they explained, was so universally detested that they were now viewed as ordinary citizens who had no right to call the Senate.

The plebeians, watching this, began to murmur to themselves about joining the Senate's rebellion. If the senators wouldn't gather for the Senate, so too would they reject the military draft and fight against being enlisted.

EXILE TO THE COUNTRYSIDE

Not only were there were no patricians in the Forum, there were also almost no patricians to be found in the City. Disgusted with the situation, the patricians had long since retreated to their country homes to focus on their own affairs, as they had been taken out of the nation's. They were distancing themselves from injury as much as they were distancing themselves from impotent masters.

When the summoned senators continued to ignore orders to assemble, messengers were sent to their homes to impose penalties for non-attendance and find out whether their absence was intentional or not. The messengers brought back the news: the senators were, indeed, out in the country. The decemvirs gave them the benefit of the doubt; being out in the country was a much better outcome than being inside the City and outright rejecting them. They ordered all the senators to be summoned for a meeting the next day.

The meeting was attended by more senators than even the decemvirs, themselves, had expected. It made the plebeians feel that their freedom was being betrayed. They saw that the senators had obeyed the orders of the decemvirs, whom they viewed as ordinary citizens, and were now giving the decemvirs the right to command them.

"TEN TARQUINS"

39. The senators demonstrated more obedience in attending the meeting than by their submissiveness in the views they shared, as I understand it.

It's documented that after a question of war had been introduced by Appius Claudius, but before formal discussion began, Lucius Valerius Potitus demanded to speak on the state of the nation first. When the decemvirs tried to silence him with threats, he declared that he would take his case to the plebeians.

We also know that Marcus Horatius Barbatus showed equal courage, labeling the decemvirs as "ten Tarquins" and reminding them that the Valerii and Horatii had driven out the kings:

The plebeians weren't disgusted by the name "king," he said. After all, it was commonly used to refer to Jupiter Optimus Maximus and it was the word by which Romulus, the City's founder, and his successors were also known. The word was even preserved in religious ceremonies. Instead, what the plebeians despised was the tyranny and violence of a king.

If such behavior was unacceptable in a king and his family, why should it be tolerated in the ex-decemvirs who are now private citizens? By suppressing free speech in the Senate, the decemvirs might force plebeians to voice their concerns outside the senate-house.

And why was it less permissible for himself, a private citizen, to call the plebeians to an assembly than for the decemvirs, who were now private citizens, to summon the Senate? The decemvirs should test, whenever they wish, how much stronger the desire to defend one's freedom is, than the desire to defend unjust domination.

The decemvirs referred to the Sabine war as if there were any war more important for the Roman plebeians to fight than a war with those who, elected to create laws, were lawless themselves and had stripped away everything of legal authority in the state. They had abolished annual elections, the annual magistrates, and the regular succession of rulers, which was the only way to ensure equal liberty. Why, despite being private citizens, did the decemvirs still hold the fasces and the power of despotic kings? After the kings were expelled, the magistrates appointed were patricians, and later, following the plebeians' secession, plebeian magistrates were appointed.

Which group did the decemvirs belong to? Were they plebeians or patricians? What had the decemvirs ever done with the plebeians' approval? If they were patricians, why had they not convened a Senate meeting for almost a year? And now that they have, they prevent many from sharing their views on the political situation.

Don't rely too heavily on the fears of others, Horatius said. The hardships men were currently enduring seemed to them much greater than any they may fear in the future.

"NO DECREE SHOULD BE PASSED"

40. While Marcus Horatius was speaking in this way, the decemvirs were paralyzed with decision about which reaction they could afford to make. Should they be angry and resistant or simply overlook what was being said? They couldn't predict the outcome of the situation.

During this time, Caius Claudius, the uncle of Appius Claudius, the decemvir, made a plea that sounded more like a request than scolding. He asked Appius to remember the society he was born into, rather than the dishonest agreement he had made with his colleagues. Caius Claudius made this plea more for Appius' sake than for the good of the City because he believed that the City would fight for its rights, with or without the decemvirs' approval. He warned that big conflicts often lead to big resentments, and it was these resentments that he worried about.

Even though the decemvirs ordered the Senate to only discuss the topic they had presented, they respected Caius Claudius too much to interrupt him. He ended his speech by offering a resolution that no decree should be passed by the Senate. Everyone understood this to mean that Claudius considered the decemvirs to be private citizens. Many of the consular rank agreed with him without discussion.

Another suggestion was made that seemed harsher but was less effective. It called for the patricians to gather to elect an interrex. By making any decision, they acknowledged that the decemvirs who called the Senate meeting were some sort of magistrates; whereas the decemvirs had been rated as mere citizens when Claudius suggested that no decision should be made.

"There Are Greater Issues Right Now"

With the decemvirs' cause already collapsing, Lucius Cornelius Maluginensis, the brother of Marcus Cornelius, the decemvir, who was saved for last among the consular men to end the debate, began to speak. He defended his brother and his colleagues by expressing concern about the war.

Cornelius wondered why the decemvirs were being attacked by those who were running for office? Why were they causing political conflict now as to who the lawful magistrates were, when the enemy was almost at the gate? Could it not wait until later, during the many months when the state wasn't busy? Was it that they were trying to hide their true intentions in the chaos? Since minds were occupied with greater matters, decisions should be set aside until there is time to regard them.

The issue Lucius Valerius and Marcus Horatius raised, that the decemvirs had left office before the Ides of May, should be discussed in the Senate after the impending wars were over and peace had been restored. Appius Claudius should be prepared to explain the election of the decemvirs, whether they were elected for one year or until the missing laws were approved.

All other issues should be put aside for now, except for the war, he said. If they believed the reports about the war were false and that not only messengers but also Tusculan ambassadors had brought inaccurate news, they should send scouts to get more accurate information. If they believed the reports and the ambassadors, they should start recruiting soldiers as soon as possible. The decemvirs should lead the armies wherever they thought was best. No other issue should be more important than this one.

ENDING THE DEBATE

41. While there was some disagreement among others, the younger patricians were in agreement.

Valerius and Horatius, with increased intensity, loudly demanded the right to share their thoughts. They threatened to go straight to the public if they weren't allowed speak to the Senate. Private individuals, whether in the Senate or in the Assembly, couldn't stop them, and they wouldn't give in to the decemvirs' imagined authority. Appius Claudius interrupted the outbursts, realizing that he needed to fight back with equal intensity. At this point, his authority was in jeopardy. "It'll be better," he said, "to not speak about any subject except the one we're considering now."

Lucius Valerius continued, loudly refusing to allow a "private citizen" to silence him. Claudius ordered a lictor to advance toward him. Valerius ran to the doors of the Senate, seeking the plebeians' protection. Lucius Cornelius immediately got up and threw his arms around Appius, pretending to side with Valerius and thus ending the argument. At Cornelius' request, Lucius Valerius was allowed to speak his mind, but this freedom didn't go beyond the boundaries they set, and the decemvirs achieved their goal.

Despite their issues with the decemvirs, the consulars and elder senators still resented the power of the tribunes. They saw that the plebeians desired the tribunes' power more than the consuls' power. The consulars and elder senators preferred that the decemvirs voluntarily give up their office in the future rather than the plebeians gaining power with the tribunes during an absence of leadership. They hoped that if the issue were handled gently, it might return the consuls to power without public unrest. The plebeians then might forget their tribunes, either due to wars or the consuls' moderate use of their power.

A DRAFT, WITH MORE CONFLICT AT HOME THAN ABROAD

A draft was announced. The patricians and decemvirs remained silent. Since there was no appeal against the command, the young men responded to their names.

After enlisting the legions, the decemvirs decided who would lead the armies and who would protect the City. The most influential decemvirs were Quintus Fabius and Appius Claudius. These two decemvirs faced a more significant conflict at home than abroad.

It was thought that Appius Claudius' aggression was better suited to quell disturbances in the City. They chose Spurius Oppius to assist Appius Claudius in protecting the City, with authority to coordinate with all the decemvirs.

Quintus Fabius' character was inconsistent and he was seen as being more inclined to evil pursuits than good ones. He was once a distinguished leader both domestically and in the military, but the decemvirate and bad influence from his colleagues had changed him to be more like Appius rather than himself. He was given the war against the Sabines, with colleagues Manius Rabuleius and Quintus Paetelius accompanying him. Marcus Cornelius was sent to Algidum with Lucius Menucius, Titus Antonius, Caeso Duillius, and Marcus Sergius.

Army Sabotages the Decemvirs

42. The military operations were no more successful in the wars with the Sabines and Aequians than domestic administration was. The only mistake made by the decemvirs was that they had made themselves despised by their fellow citizens.

Otherwise, the blame rested entirely with the soldiers. The soldiers allowed themselves to be defeated to ensure that no mission would succeed under the leadership of the decemvirs, to their own humiliation and that of the decemvirs. The Roman armies were defeated by the Sabines at Eretum and by the Aequians in Algidum.

After fleeing from Eretum under the cover of night, the Romans arrived at a previously fortified camp between Fidenae and Crustumeria, closer to Rome. The Roman soldiers didn't engage the Sabines who pursued them, but instead fortified the camp using the natural advantages of the high ground and entrenchments to protect them, not their courage or weapons.

In Algidum, the Romans suffered greater humiliation and defeat by the Aequians, even going so far as to lose their camp. The Roman soldiers, devoid of all their equipment, sought refuge in Tusculum, relying on the goodwill and mercy of their hosts for survival, which they did receive. The news that reached Rome was so alarming that, with their hatred for the decemvirs set aside, the senators decided to keep watch in the City. They ordered all those of suitable age to carry arms to stand guard on the City walls and establish outposts at the gates. The senators also decided to send weapons and reinforcements to Tusculum. The senators ordered the decemvirs to leave the Tusculum citadel and keep their troops encamped.

The other camp was to be moved from Fidenae into Sabine territory. The hope was that, by striking first, the Sabines would be discouraged from planning an attack on the City.

Chapter 12

THE TERRIBLE ACTS OF THE DECEMVIRS (449 BC)

43. THE DECEMVIRS ADDED two terrible acts to the disasters caused by the enemy, one abroad and one inside the City.

THE FIRST TERRIBLE ACT: SICCIUS

In the Sabine region, a Roman leader named Lucius Siccius was believed to have secretly discussed the decemvirs' envy of tribunes and sowing ideas of secession with a crowd of soldiers. So, as a ruse, the decemvirs sent him ahead to choose a campsite. The soldiers who were sent with him were instructed to attack and kill him whenever the opportunity arose. However, the soldiers didn't kill him without consequence for some fell around him and died while Siccius, a man of great strength and courage, defended himself.

The remaining soldiers returned to the camp and reported that Siccius had been ambushed while fighting bravely, and some soldiers had died with him. At first, everyone believed their story. But later, a group of soldiers who had been allowed by the decemvirs to bury the dead noticed that none of the bodies had been stripped of their belongings. And Lucius Siccius was found in the center, surrounded by the bodies of the fallen soldiers, all facing him. There were no Sabine bodies or signs of their retreat. The soldiers brought back Siccius' body, claiming that he had been killed by his own men.

The news filled the camp with outrage. There were plans to bring Lucius Siccius' body back to Rome immediately, but the decemvirs quickly arranged a military funeral for him at public expense. He was buried amidst the soldiers' deep sorrow, and the decemvirs' reputation among the plebeians was severely damaged.

THE SECOND TERRIBLE ACT: VERGINIA

44. The second terrible act occurred in the City, born out of brutal lust, leading to consequences as tragic as the event that expelled the Tarquins from the City and throne due to the rape and violent death of Lucretia. Similarly, the decemvirs lost their power in the same way and for the same reasons as Rome's kings did.

Appius Claudius developed an unlawful desire to violate a young woman of plebeian status, named Verginia. The girl's father, Lucius Verginius, was a respected centurion at Algidum, known for his exemplary conduct both at home and in the military. His wife had been properly educated and his children were raised well. He had promised Verginia in marriage to Lucius Icilius, a former tribune known for his courage and dedication to the plebeians.

Consumed by desire for the beautiful young girl, Appius Claudius tried to win her over with bribes and promises. When he realized that her modesty prevented him from possessing her, he finally resorted to cruel and tyrannical force. He ordered his client, Marcus Claudius, to claim the girl as his slave and to resist anyone who might demand her temporary freedom. Appius took this opportunity to take her as her father was away.

When the girl came to the Forum, where there were games in the booths, Marcus Claudius grabbed her and called her the daughter of his slave and a slave herself. He ordered her to follow him, threatening to drag her by force her if she resisted. The frightened girl, paralyzed by the cries of her nurse pleading for help, attracted a crowd. The respected names of her father, Verginius, and her betrothed, Icilius, were on everyone's lips. Friends came to her aid, won over by their respect for them, while the indignation of the people and their sympathy for the maiden helped her.

Marcus Claudius told the crowd that there was no need for a mob; he was merely acting within the law, not using force, and the woman was safe. He summoned her to court. Those who were with her advised her to follow him, and they arrived at Appius Claudius' tribunal. Marcus Claudius repeated the false story to Appius Claudius, now the judge as well as the mastermind of the plot. He claimed that a girl born in his house had been abducted and secretly moved to Verginius' house and had been passed off as the latter's daughter. He claimed that he had solid evidence and would prove it even to Verginius, who would be most affected by the loss. Marcus Claudius argued that it was only fair that the girl should stay with her master in the meantime.

The advocates for Verginia argued that Verginius was away on state business, that he would be back in two days if they sent word to him, and that it was unfair for him to risk losing his children while he was away. The advocates asked that the whole matter be postponed until the father's arrival, that the girl be allowed temporary freedom according to the law passed by Appius Claudius himself, and that a young woman of marriageable age not be forced to risk her reputation before her freedom.

OUTRAGE AND DISGUST

45. Appius Claudius began his decree by noting that the law, which Verginia's friends were using as the basis of their request, clearly demonstrated his support for Verginia's freedom. However, he stated that this freedom would only be safeguarded if it didn't change depending on the situation or the people involved. The law, he argued, was valid only for those who were claimed to be free, as anyone could legally represent them. But Verginia was either under her father's control or a slave under the control of her master. She wasn't free and no action to recover her freedom was necessary.

Appius decided that Verginia's father should be summoned. In the meantime, Marcus Claudius, the claimant, wouldn't lose his rights and could take the girl with him, promising to bring her back when her father arrived. This decision was met with murmurs of disapproval, but no one dared to openly object.

Verginia's uncle, Publius Numitorius, and her betrothed, Lucius Icilius, arrived. The crowd made way for them, thinking that Appius Claudius could be best opposed by Icilius. When Icilius tried to speak, a lictor announced that the matter had been decided and pushed the shouting Icilius aside. Angered by the injustice, Icilius declared, "I'm, by your orders, Appius, to be removed from here at the point of the sword. You may stifle all comment on what you want to keep concealed. However, I'm going to marry this girl, and I'm determined to have a chaste wife. Summon all the lictors of all your colleagues and give orders for the axes and rods to be ready. The betrothed of Icilius shall not remain outside her father's house. Even if you have deprived us of the two foundations of our liberty, the aid of our tribunes and the right of appeal to the Roman plebeians, you have no right to our wives and children, the victims of your lust."

"Vent your cruelty upon our backs and necks, but let female honor at least be safe! If any violence happens to this girl, I will invoke the aid of the Roman citizens here for the woman betrothed to me. Lucius Verginius will get aid similarly for his only daughter, except with soldiers! We shall all ask for the aid of gods and men, and you'll never carry out this judgment except by killing us all. Reflect, Appius. Where are you going with this? When Verginius comes, he must decide what action to take. If he submits to this man's claim, then he must look for another husband for her. As for me, in defense of the freedom of my bride, I'll sooner die than prove disloyal."

"I AM SO THANKFUL FOR YOUR HELP"

46. The crowd was now stirred up, and it seemed like a conflict was about to break out. The lictors had positioned themselves around Lucius Icilius, but they didn't take any action beyond making threats.

Appius said that Lucius Icilius wasn't defending Verginia. Instead, as a restless man with a desire for power, Icilius was merely looking for a reason to cause trouble. He wouldn't give Icilius satisfaction today and wouldn't be giving in to Icilius' demands. Rather, he would honor the absent Verginius and the concept of fatherhood and freedom. Therefore, he wouldn't make a decision today, nor would he issue a decree. He asked Marcus Claudius to give up some of his rights and allow the girl to be released the next day. However, if the father didn't show up the next day, he warned Icilius and his supporters, he wouldn't hesitate to enforce his own law. And he wouldn't need the help of his colleagues' lictors to suppress the agitators; his own lictors would be enough.

When the unjust act was postponed and Verginia's supporters had left, it was decided that Icilius' brother and Numitorius' son, both energetic young men, should go straight to the gates of the camp and bring Lucius Verginius as quickly as possible. Verginia's safety depended on him being there the next day to protect her. They quickly left, and riding at full speed brought the news to the father.

Meanwhile, Marcus Claudius still claimed Verginia and was collecting sureties. He was also pressuring Icilius to defend himself and provide sureties. Icilius told him that was exactly what he was doing, intentionally delaying the proceedings to give the messengers sent to the camp to fetch Verginius enough time for their journey. The crowd raised their hands in support of Icilius, and everyone was ready to vouch for him. With tears in his eyes he said, "I'm so thankful for your help. I'll need your help tomorrow. For now, I have enough sureties." Thus, Verginia was released on the pledges of her relatives.

Not wanting to seem like he was only there for this case, Appius Claudius remained on the bench for a while. When no one else came forward, he went home and wrote to his colleagues at Verginius' camp, instructing them not to give Verginius a leave of absence and to keep him under guard. However, this evil plan was too late, as Verginius, having set out after gathering provisions, had already left during the first watch of the night. The letter regarding his detention arrived the next morning, but it was too late.

A FATHER APPEALS TO THE PEOPLE

47. In the City, the citizens gathered in the Forum, waiting in anticipation. Lucius Verginius, dressed in rags of mourning, led his daughter, also in rags of mourning, into the square at dawn. They were accompanied by a group of matrons also in rags and a large number of supporters.

Lucius Verginius began to move among the people and to detain individuals, asking for their help. He didn't just request their assistance as a favor, but claimed it as his right, reminding them that he fought daily in battle to protect their children and spouses, and that no other man had performed more courageous acts in war than he. What good is it if, with the City safe, your children should suffer as if the City had been captured? He circulated around the people, almost speaking in a public address, but he spoke to them one by one. Lucius Icilius used similar arguments, but the women's silent weeping was more powerful than any words.

Despite all this, Appius Claudius, driven more by madness of lust than love, took his place on the judge's stand. Marcus Claudius, the man working for Appius and falsely claiming the girl, began to complain that he hadn't received justice the day before due to partiality.

Before he could complete his request or Verginius could be given a chance to respond, Appius interrupted. The introduction to what was said next, his judgement, may have been recorded accurately by ancient authors, but because I find no likely introduction for such a disgraceful matter, it seems best to simply state the fact that no one disputes: Appius Claudius declared the girl a slave.

At first, everyone was shocked by this outrageous act, and a silence fell over the crowd. When Marcus Claudius pushed through the crowd and tried to take the girl, the women surrounding her began to cry out in sorrow. Verginius, pointing threateningly at Appius, declared, "It's to Icilius and not to you, Appius, that I've betrothed my daughter; I've brought her up for marriage, not for rape. Are you determined to satisfy your brutal lusts, just like cattle and wild beasts, to rush promiscuously into intercourse? Whether these people will put up with this, I don't know, but I hope that those who possess weapons will refuse to do so."

When Marcus Claudius was pushed back by the crowd of matrons and supporters surrounding her, the herald called for silence.

"IS THIS THE REWARD FOR OUR CHILDREN'S VIRTUE?"

48. Appius Claudius, his mind still consumed by lust, claimed that he had hard evidence of a planned rebellion. This evidence came not only from these harsh words of Lucius Icilius and the actions of Lucius Verginius, which were witnessed by all of Rome, but also from other, reliable sources. He learned that secret meetings were held throughout the night to incite a rebellion. In fact, He brought armed soldiers with him, not to harm peaceful citizens, but to punish those who threatened the peace of the state."

"Therefore, it's better to be quiet," he said. "Lictor, remove the crowd and clear the way for the master to seize the slave!" After he finished his rage-filled words, the crowd itself moved aside, and the girl, abandoned as plunder, stood there.

Then Verginius, seeing no help anywhere, said, "I beg you, Appius, first forgive my fatherly grief if I've spoken to you harshly; and then allow me to question the nurse in front of the virgin to understand what this is all about, so that if I've been falsely accused as the father, I may leave here with a clear conscience."

After getting permission, he took Verginia and the nurse aside to the booths near the temple of Cloacina, now known as the "New Booths." There, he grabbed a knife from a butcher and plunged the knife into Verginia's breast saying, "This is the only way I can ensure your freedom." Then, looking back at the tribunal, he cursed Appius Claudius saying, "By this blood, Appius, I devote your head to the infernal gods."

Appius, shocked by the horrific act, immediately ordered Verginius to be arrested. But Verginius, armed with the knife, fought his way through the crowd protected by a large group of sympathizers and escaped. Icilius and Numitorius picked up Verginia's lifeless body and showed it to the people, lamenting Appius' cruelty, the girl's tragic beauty, and the desperate act of her father.

Everyone was affected. The matrons in the crowd cried out, "Is this the price of raising children and the reward for maintaining their virtue?" Their grief was intense, and their words were deeply moving. The voices of the men, led by Icilius, focused their anger on the abolition of the tribune power, the loss of their right to appeal, and their indignation at the disrespect shown to the state.

FLEEING WITH HIS TOGA OVER HIS HEAD

49. The crowd was stirred up, both by the horrific nature of the act and by the opportunity of regaining their freedom. Appius then commanded Lucius Icilius to be brought before him, and when he refused to come, ordered him to be arrested.

Eventually, when the officers couldn't get to him, Appius himself, accompanied by a group of young patricians, entered the crowd and ordered the lictor to drag Icilius to prison in chains. By now, not only the crowd, but also Lucius Valerius and Marcus Horatius, the leaders of the crowd, stood by Icilius. They pushed back the lictor of the decemvirs, declaring that if Appius was acting legally, Lucius Icilius was a private citizen, and they had a right to defend him. If Appius wanted to use force, they would be a good match for him. This led to a violent struggle. The lictor of the decemvir attacked Valerius and Horatius, but the crowd smashed the lictor's fasces.

Appius Claudius climbed the tribunal to address the people, followed by Horatius and Valerius. The assembly listened to Horatius and Valerius but drowned out the voice of Appius Claudius with their shouts when he tried to speak. And now, in accordance with his authority, Valerius then ordered the lictors to leave Lucius Icilius and cease guarding Appius Claudius, as he was merely a private citizen. Appius Claudius, his spirit broken and now fearing for his life, ran into a house near the Forum, his head covered with his toga, where he hid from his opponents.

Spurius Oppius, trying to help Appius, as he was his colleague, ran into the Forum from the other side. He saw their authority being overpowered by the force of the people. Distracted by conflicting advice coming from many sides, he finally ordered the Senate to be convened. This calmed the plebeians, as they knew the actions of the decemvirs were disliked by most of the patricians, and the plebeians hoped that the Senate would end the power of the decemvirs.

The Senate decided that the plebeians shouldn't be provoked and that what was more important was that precautions should be taken not to cause any disturbance at camp when Verginius arrived.

50. Some of the younger patricians were sent to the camp on Mount Vecilius, tasked with informing the three decemvirs who were in command that the decemvirs were to prevent the soldiers from rebelling.

"WE ARE MEN, AND WE ARE ARMED."

However, when he arrived back at camp, Verginius caused an even greater commotion than the one he left in the City. He arrived with nearly four-hundred men from Rome who joined him as companions from the City, outraged by the recent events. His bloody appearance, still gripping the knife, alarmed the soldiers. Moreover, the sight of so many togas seen in the camp created the appearance of a much larger City crowd than it actually was. When asked what had happened, Verginius wept. He was too upset to say anything. Finally, when the noise of the approaching crowd subsided and there was silence, he explained everything in the order that it had happened.

Holding his hands out to appeal, he pleaded with his fellow soldiers not to blame him for the crime committed by Appius Claudius or shun him as a murderer. He said that he would have valued his daughter's life more highly if she had been allowed to live free and chaste. Since he saw her being dragged off like a slave for the sole purpose of raping her, he considered it better for her to die than to suffer for the rest of her life. His feeling of pity led him into a semblance of cruelty. He would have taken his own life too, if he hadn't had the hope of avenging her death with the help of his fellow soldiers. For they, too, have daughters, sisters, and wives. Raping his daughter wouldn't have quenched Appius Claudius' lust. His lawlessness would continue if he knew he could continue to get away with it in the future without any punishment.

The calamity would as a warning to the men listening, so that they could avoid similar injustices. As for himself, his wife was deceased, and his daughter, since she wouldn't live any longer in chastity, had met a miserable but honorable death. There was no longer anyone in his home for Appius Claudius' lust: he would defend himself with the same spirit with which he defended his daughter. Others, he said, should take care of themselves and their own children similarly.

The crowd responded with a promise to support Verginius, pledging that they wouldn't fail to avenge his grief or assert their own freedom. The toga-wearing citizens mixed with the soldiers shared their own stories of outrageous occurrences in Rome, further fueling the soldiers' anger and a general impression that the decemvirs' power had already been overthrown in Rome. Then others claimed that Appius had been nearly killed and had gone into exile. This caused a call to arms, urging standards to be taken out and a march back to Rome.

The three decemvirs, disturbed both by what they saw and by what they heard had happened in Rome, dispersed in different directions within the camp to calm the disturbances. As long as they spoke in a mildly reproaching manner, they were met with no response. If they tried to speak with authority, the soldiers responded, "We're men and we're armed."

NO LACK OF ANSWERS, A LACK OF LEADERSHIP

The army marched in formation to Rome and positioned themselves on the Aventine Hill, urging the plebeians, as they fell in with them, to reclaim their freedom and elect plebeian tribunes. No calls for violence were heard.

In response, Spurius Oppius called the Senate together. The Senate decided not to take harsh action, recognizing that the decemvirs were to blame for the rebellion. With the Senate's authority, three former consuls, Spurius Tarpeius, Caius Julius, and Publius Sulpicius were sent to inquire by whose order the camp had been deserted, abandoning the enemy, and why had they besieged the Aventine Hill capturing their City.

There was no lack of answers. There was a lack of someone to give a response, as there was no clear leader yet or no one was sufficiently daring to offer themselves up. Finally, the multitude shouted that Lucius Valerius and Marcus Horatius should be sent to them: they would give their response to these men.

A NEW TYPE OF TRIBUNE: MILITARY TRIBUNES

51. After the ambassadors left, Lucius Verginius spoke to the soldiers. He reminded them that they had struggled with a relative-

ly simple issue, just minutes earlier, because they lacked leadership. Their solution, while not bad, was more the result of chance than a well-thought-out plan.

Verginius suggested that the soldiers elect ten people to lead them, and that these leaders should be given the title of "Military Tribunes" with military honor. When the soldiers offered him the honor of being one of the military tribunes, Verginius declined. "Save your high opinion of me for a better time. I can't accept any honor until my daughter is avenged. In the current chaotic situation, it wouldn't be helpful for you to have leaders who are targets of political hatred. I can be useful to you even if I'm not in a leadership position." The soldiers then elected ten military tribunes.

Meanwhile, the Roman army sent to fight the Sabines was also active. There, Lucius Icilius and Publius Numitorius led a rebellion against those decemvirs. The soldiers, still angry about the murder of Lucius Siccius, were further enraged by this news of a brutal attack on a young girl. When Icilius heard that the soldiers with Verginius on Mount Aventine had elected their own ten military tribunes, he worried that the plebeians might follow their example and elect the same people as tribunes. To prevent this, he made sure that his own soldiers elected ten military tribunes with equal power before they went to Rome.

The soldiers then entered the City through the Colline Gate in a military formation and marched through the heart of the City to the Aventine Hill. There, they joined the other army and asked the twenty military tribunes to choose two of them to be the main commanders. They chose Marcus Oppius and Sextus Manilius.

The patricians, fearing for the safety of Rome, met every day but spent more time arguing than making decisions. The decemvirs were charged with the murder of Siccius, the lust of Appius Claudius, and the military failures.

The patricians decided that the ambassadors, Lucius Valerius and Marcus Horatius, should go to the Aventine Hill, but Valerius and Horatius refused to go unless the decemvirs gave up their office, which had officially ended the previous year. The decemvirs complained that they were being unfairly treated and insisted that they wouldn't resign until the laws for which they had been appointed were passed.

An Empty City Holds No Power

52. Marcus Duillius, a former tribune, told the plebeians that their constant disputes were preventing any work from being done in the Senate. Duillius believed that the patricians wouldn't take their responsibilities seriously until they saw Rome deserted. He suggested the plebeians move from the Aventine Hill, inside Rome, to the Sacred Mount outside the City. Dullius thought that the Sacred Mount would remind them of the plebeian's determination and that the patricians would realize that harmony couldn't be restored without reinstating the tribune's power.

Following this advice, the armies set off along the Nomentan, then known as the Ficulan Road, and set up camp on the Sacred Mount. They committed no acts of violence, following the example of their ancestors. The plebeians followed the army, with only those too old to travel staying behind. Their wives and children accompanied them, asking who would protect them in a city where neither purity nor freedom were respected.

When everything in Rome had become desolate and unfamiliar due to the solitude, there was no one in the Forum except for a few old men. The Forum, having been deserted, then appeared empty when the Senators were summoned to the Senate.

There were many others besides Horatius and Valerius who protested. "What are you waiting for, senators?" they cried. "If the decemvirs don't end their stubbornness, will you let everything fall into chaos? What power do you hold, decemvirs, if you only rule over empty buildings? Are you not embarrassed that there are more of your lictors than citizens in togas in the Forum? What will you do if an enemy approaches the City? What if the plebeians return armed? Do you plan to end your rule with the fall of the City?"

"You can either not have plebeians or have plebeians and accept their tribunes. You can't have both. We would rather do without our patrician magistrates than they without their plebeian magistrates. The plebeians took this power from our ancestors when it was offered, new and untested; the plebeians won't tolerate losing it now that they have experienced its benefits, especially since we haven't used our power moderately, so the plebeians need the help of the tribunes."

THE DECEMVIRS STEP DOWN

When these arguments were made from all sides, the decemvirs, overwhelmed by the unanimous opinion, agreed to step down and submit to the authority of the Senate. The decemvirs only asked for one thing, and it was also a warning: they wanted protection from the anger of the plebeians. If the patricians allowed them to shed the blood of the decemvirs, it set precedent that the same could be done to the patricians.

53. Lucius Valerius and Marcus Horatius were sent as ambassadors to negotiate with the plebeians and resolve their differences. They were also tasked with protecting the decemvirs from the anger and

potential violence of the crowd. The plebeians welcomed them into the camp with great joy, recognizing them as champions of liberty both at the start of the disturbance and in its aftermath. Valerius and Horatius were thanked upon their arrival, with Lucius Icilius speaking on behalf of the plebeians.

When the negotiations began, the ambassadors asked what the plebeians wanted. Icilius, who had already planned out their demands, made it clear that the plebeians were relying more on the justice of their cause than on force. The plebeians wanted the return of the tribunes and the right of appeal, which had been their safeguards before the decemvirs were appointed. They also wanted assurance that no one would be punished for encouraging the soldiers or the plebeians to fight for their freedom. Their only excessive demand was for the punishment of the decemvirs; the plebeians wanted them handed over and threatened to burn them alive.

A WARNING AGAINST REVENGE

To these proposals, the commissioners replied:

"The demands you have made are so reasonable that they should have been granted voluntarily. You seek assurances of liberty, not permission to attack others. But your anger is more to be forgiven rather than to be indulged, since hatred of cruelty is pushing you into cruelty, and almost before you are free yourselves, you are seeking to dominate your adversaries."

"Will there never be a time when our state will be free from executions inflicted either by the patricians on the Roman plebeians or by the plebeians on the patricians? You need protection more than aggression. It should be more than sufficient for a common citizen to live enjoying equal rights in the state without causing or suffering harm. Even if you are to become feared one day, when you have regained your magistrates and laws and have the authority to judge us on our lives and fortunes, you'll then decide each case according to its merits. For now, it's enough to recover your liberty."

Chapter 13

RETURN OF THE CONSULS (449 BC)

54. WHEN THE PLEBEIANS unanimously gave the ambassadors freedom to act as they saw fit, the ambassadors promised to return quickly once they had settled matters. The ambassadors then departed and explained the plebeians' message to the patricians. The decemvirs, surprised that there was no talk of any kind of punishment, didn't object to anything.

Appius Claudius, measuring the hatred of others by his own hatred toward them, knew that he and his hard-hearted nature were particularly disliked. He anticipated the hostility toward him, saying, "I know what awaits me. I understand that the fight against us is postponed until we hand over our weapons. The plebeians' anger will demand a sacrifice. So, I'm ready to give up my position as decemvir."

DECEMVIRS DISSOLVED

The Senate then passed a decree. The decemvirs were to resign immediately. Quintus Furius, the Pontifex Maximus, was to hold an election for tribunes. No one was to be punished for the soldiers and plebeians' secession. After these decrees were passed and the Senate was dismissed, the decemvirs formally resigned their positions in front of the assembly, to the great joy of all.

The news was reported back to the plebeians on the Sacred Mount, and whomever remained inside the City escorted the ambassadors back to the camp where they were met by a happy crowd. The restoration of freedom and unity to the state was at hand. The ambassadors then addressed the people:

"Prosperity, favor, and good fortune to you and the Republic! Return to your homes, your household gods, your wives, and your children. But bring the same respect you showed here back into the City. Go back to the Aventine Hill, where you started. In that auspicious place, where you first sought freedom, you'll elect tribunes. The Pontifex Maximus will be there to hold the elections."

The plebeians agreed and were overjoyed. They quickly uprooted their standards and headed for Rome, celebrating with everyone they met. In silence, the people marched under arms through the City until they reached the Aventine Hill. There, the Pontifex Maximus immediately held the election of the tribunes. They elected Lucius Verginius, Lucius Icilius, and Publius Numitorius, the uncle of Verginia, as their tribunes. They were the ones who organized the secession. Then they elected Caius Sicinius, the son of the first tribune elected on the Sacred Mount, and Marcus Duillius, who had been a distinguished tribune before the decemvirs were created and always supported the plebeians during the decemvirs' disputes. Marcus Titinius, Marcus Pomponius, Caius Apronius, Publius Villius, and Caius Oppius were elected based on hope for their future usefulness rather than past service.

RETURN OF THE CONSULS

Once the election was over, Lucius Icilius proposed to the plebeians, and the plebeians agreed, that no one should be harmed because of the secession from the decemvirs. Promptly, Marcus Duillius then proposed a measure to elect consuls with the right of appeal. All these measures were passed in a council of the plebeians in the Flaminian Meadows, now known as the Circus Flaminius.

55. Then, through an interrex, Lucius Valerius Publicola Potitus and Marcus Horatius Turrinus Barbatus were chosen as consuls. The consuls began their duties immediately. Their leadership was well-received by the plebeians, though not by the patricians even though no injustice was inflicted upon them. The patricians felt that any measures taken to protect the freedom of the plebeians reduced their own power.

STRENGTHENING THE RIGHTS OF THE PEOPLE

The first issue was whether the patricians were obligated to follow rules made by the plebeians' assembly. Consul Valerius and Consul Horatius proposed a law at the Centuriate Comitia stating that any decisions made by the plebeians would apply to everyone. This law gave more power to the tribunes, who could propose motions.

Another consular law was reinstated and strengthened about the right to appeal, which had been undermined by the decemvirs' power. The new law stated that no one could elect a magistrate whose authority couldn't be appealed. If someone did, it was legal to kill them, and this act wouldn't be considered a capital crime.

After strengthening the rights of the plebeians with the right to appeal on one hand and the of the tribunes on the other, the consuls also protected the tribunes. They revived old ceremonies to remind plebeians that tribunes were sacred and untouchable, a status almost forgotten. The consuls made a law stating that anyone who harmed a tribune, plebeian aedile, or judges of the decemvirs, his head would be cut off and consecrated to Jupiter Optimus Maximus, his property would be sold, and his family would be sold into slavery at the Temples of Ceres, Liber, or Libera. According to this law, legal interpreters deny that anyone is sacred and untouchable, but that whomever harms any of them would have his head cut off and consecrated to Jupiter; thus, it's argued that an aedile can be arrested and imprisoned by higher magistrates, which may be illegal (as it isn't permissible to harm an aedile under this law) and he doesn't count as being sacred and untouchable. The old law had sworn that the tribunes, from the moment they were first appointed, were sacred and untouchable. Some interpreted that by the same Horatian law, consuls and praetors were also included, as they were elected with the same auspices as the consuls, since the judge was referred to as a consul. This interpretation is refuted, as at that time it was customary to call a praetor a judge, not a consul. These were the consular laws enacted.

The same consuls also decided that the Senate's decrees should be kept with the plebeian aediles in the Temple of Ceres. Before this, the consuls could illegally change or hide these decisions.

Marcus Duillius, a tribune, proposed a law that anyone who left the plebeians without representation by the tribunes or caused a magistrate to be elected without the right to appeal should be whipped and beheaded.

All these changes were made against the wishes of the patricians, but the patricians didn't oppose them because no specific person was targeted.

APPIUS USES APPEALS HE TRIED REMOVING

56. The power of the tribunes and the freedom of the plebeians were now firmly in place. The tribunes felt it was the right time to bring

charges against individuals. The tribunes chose Lucius Verginius to be the first prosecutor and Appius Claudius as the defendant. Verginius set a date for Appius to appear in court. When Appius arrived at the Forum with a group of young patricians, everyone was reminded of his past abuses of power as they saw him and his bodyguards.

Verginius then spoke, "Long speeches are usually used when there is doubt. I don't want to waste time talking about Appius' guilt, as everyone already knows about his cruel actions. I don't want to let Appius defend himself with an impudent defense of his crimes. Therefore, Appius Claudius, I grant you grace for all the crimes that you have dared to commit over the past two years impiously and wickedly. I've decided to focus on one charge against you. I accuse Appius of sentencing a free person to slavery, which is against the law." Verginius formally offered Appius a chance to prove his innocence by saying, "Unless you name a judge before whom you can prove your innocence, I shall order you to be taken in chains to prison."

Appius had no hope of getting help from the tribunes or the plebeians. He tried to appeal to the tribunes, but no one listened to him. When he was taken by the bailiff, he shouted, "I appeal." Everyone was shocked to hear this phrase, which is usually used to protect freedom, coming from the man who had recently sentenced a free citizen to slavery. The crowd grew silent.

Then the plebeians started to mumble saying that there must be gods who care about human affairs. Punishment for tyranny and cruelty may come late, but it's never light. How ironic that Appius Claudius appeals for help when he had crushed our right to appeal! And he's asking for the plebeians' protection when he had denied protection to us. See how he's being taken to prison without any rights, just like he had sentenced a free person to slavery without the right to defend themselves!

Amid the murmurs of the crowd, Appius pleaded for the Roman people to remember his ancestor's service to the state, both at home and in war, and his own unfortunate zeal for the Roman plebeians when he, for the sake of equalizing the laws, greatly offended the patricians who removed him from his position as consul. He declared that those laws, if maintained, were still in effect, and will lead him to be taken to prison in chains. Furthermore, when he has a chance to present his case, he will test both his own good and bad deeds. For now, as a Roman citizen, he asked for the right to speak on the appointed day and to appeal to the judgment of the plebeians. He wasn't so terrified by hatred that he had no hope in the fairness and compassion of his fellow citizens.

But if, without a trial, he was taken to prison without being heard, he would again appeal to the tribunes and warn them not to imitate those they hate. If the tribunes admit being bound by the same agreement of cancelling the right of appeal which they accused the decemvirs of doing, he would then appeal to the plebeians. He asked for the protection of the laws that had just been passed this year, by both the consuls and tribunes, which allowed for the right to appeal. What was the point of an appeal if a man, not yet found guilty, couldn't make it? If he, Appius Claudius, can't find protection in the laws, then no plebeian can. His case would show whether the new laws promoted domination or freedom, and whether the right to appeal and challenge the injustice of the magistrates was just an empty promise or a real right.

THE CASE AGAINST APPIUS CLAUDIUS

57. Lucius Verginius argued that Appius Claudius, as an expert in laws, was the only person who didn't deserve to participate in the laws or in civil or human society.

He urged the plebeians to look at the tribunal, a stronghold of all wrongdoings where that perpetual decemvir abused his power by harming the citizens' properties, bodies, and lives of citizens. Accompanied by executioners, not lictors, he threatened everyone with his rods and axes, showing no respect for gods or men. Appius then shifted his focus from theft and murder to lust, taking a free-born girl from her father's arms, treating her like a war prisoner, and giving her to a client who would have delivered her to his own bedchamber. He used a cruel decree and a terrible decision to force the girl's father to harm her. He ordered the girl's betrothed and uncle to be taken to prison when they tried to lift her lifeless body. Then, he was more upset about the interruption to his pleasure than her premature death. Finally, he also had a prison built for his own purposes, which he called the "Home of the Roman Plebeians." Therefore, Verginius argued, even if he appeals again and again, he should be brought to judgment again and again unless he gives up his right to appeal. And if he refuses to go before a judge, he should be taken away in chains to prison as someone who has been found guilty.

Appius Claudius was put in prison and, although no one disapproved, the public was greatly affected. The punishment of such a prominent man made the plebeians feel that it was an excessive use of their own freedoms to punish such a powerful man. The tribune set a date for the trial.

Meanwhile, ambassadors from the Hernicians and Latins came to Rome to congratulate them on the harmony between the patricians and plebeians. They brought a small golden crown to Jupiter Optimus Maximus, on the Capitoline Hill as a gift. They weren't wealthy, so they observed the religious rites more piously than magnificently. The ambassadors also reported that the Aequians and Volscians were preparing for war.

The consuls were ordered to divide the provinces between them. Marcus Horatius got the Sabines, and Lucius Valerius got the Aequians and Volscians. When the consuls announced a draft for these wars, the plebeians showed so much goodwill that not only the young men but also many veterans who had already served their time, volunteered. This made the army stronger in both number and quality. Before they left the City, they had the decemviral laws, known as the "Twelve Tables," engraved on bronze and displayed them publicly. Some plebeians say that the aediles did this by order of the tribunes.

THE POWER TO FORGIVE (OR NOT)

58. Caius Claudius, who had left Rome due to his disgust at the actions of the decemvirs and was particularly offended by the tyrannical conduct and arrogance of his nephew, Appius, returned from his ancestral home in Regillum. Despite his old age, he came back to plead for his nephew, whose behavior he had previously avoided. Disguised and dressed in mourning clothes, he walked around the Forum with his family and clients, asking individual citizens for their support. He pleaded with them not to tarnish the Claudian family's reputation by imprisoning one of their own. He implored them to remember that his nephew, a man who would have been honored in the highest esteem by future generations, a lawgiver and founder of Roman law, is now chained up like a criminal among thieves, bandits, and murderers.

He also asked them to set aside their anger and consider the situation carefully. Caius Claudius hoped that they would forgive his nephew due to the contributions of the Claudian family, and not to let their hatred for one man override their compassion. He admitted that he was doing this out of loyalty to his family, and not because he, himself, had forgiven his nephew. By courage, they had regained their liberty; by showing mercy, they had the power to establish harmony between the classes. Some plebeians were moved by his devotion to his family, rather than his nephew's plight.

VERGINIA'S FINAL PEACE

With tears in his eyes, Lucius Verginius begged for pity for his daughter rather than himself. He urged them to listen to the pleas of Verginia's relatives, close friends and the three tribunes, who were supposed to protect the plebeians but now needed their help. They shouldn't be heeding the pleas of the Claudian family, whose role is to tyrannize the plebeians. Verginius' tears seemed more just.

Appius Claudius, having lost hope, committed suicide the day before his trial.

Soon after, Spurius Oppius, next in unpopularity because he had been in Rome when Appius Claudius made his unjust verdict, was arrested by Publius Numitorius. However, Oppius was hated more for his own unjust actions than for not stopping Appius. A witness was brought forward who had served in twenty-seven years of military campaigns and had been honored eight times for conspicuous bravery. He showed the citizens his back, which was scarred from being whipped, and challenged Oppius that if he could name one thing he had done wrong to deserve such punishment, he would allow him, without complaint, to vent his anger upon him again. Oppius was also imprisoned and committed suicide before his trial.

The tribunes seized the property of Appius Claudius and Spurius Oppius. Their colleagues in the decemvirate left their homes and went into exile, and their property was also seized. Marcus Claudius, who had claimed Verginia as his property, was found guilty on the day of his trial. But at Verginius' request, the extreme penalty was cancelled; he was released and went into exile in Tibur.

After all the guilty parties had been punished, Verginia's spirit could finally rest in peace.

No More Trials, No More Imprisonments

59. The patricians were greatly alarmed. The expressions on the tribunes' faces had become as menacing as those of the decemvirs had been, when Marcus Duillius, a tribune of the plebeians, put a stop to their excessive power.

Dullius said, "The freedoms we have and the punishment from our enemies has gone far enough. Therefore, for this year, I won't allow a trial day to be set for anyone, nor will I allow anyone to be taken in chains. I don't want old, forgotten crimes to be brought up again, especially since the recent ones have been paid for with the punishment of the decemvirs. The constant vigilance of both consuls in protecting freedom is enough assurance that nothing will happen that will require tribune intervention."

This moderation by the tribune initially removed the fear from the senators, but it increased the anger toward the consuls. It was evident that the consuls had been so attentive to the plebeians that their care for the safety and freedom of the patricians was secondary to their concern for the plebeian magistrates. Moreover, it seemed that the consuls were more eager to ensure forgiveness for their own mistakes than to forgive the mistakes of their enemies.

Many said that the decision was milder, as the patricians had been authors of the laws enacted by the decemvirs, and there was no doubt that they had succumbed to the chaotic state of the republic.

Chapter 14

ROME BUILDS BACK (449-447 BC)

60. AFTER SETTLING THE business in the City and firmly establishing the rights of the plebeians, the consuls left for their respective provinces.

CONSUL VALERIUS GOES TO WAR

Consul Valerius wisely postponed any military actions against the combined forces of the Aequians and the Volscians at Algidum. Had he rushed into battle, the outcome might have been disastrous for the Romans, who were then under the control of the decemvirs. Valerius set up his camp a thousand paces away from the enemy and kept his men under control.

The enemy then quickly filled the space between their two camps with an army, arranged in battle formation, armed and ready for battle. The Romans didn't respond to their challenge. Eventually, the Aequians and Volscians, bored and exhausted from standing and waiting in vain for the battle, believed it to be almost a victory. So, they left the area to raid Hernician and Latin territories, leaving their camp with just enough men for defense but not enough for a full battle.

Seeing this, Valerius rallied his men and formed a battle line, now challenging the enemy to fight. The enemy declined, aware of their reduced strength, to the delight of the Romans. Morale in the Roman camp grew as the Romans saw the enemy, now fearful behind their own palisades, as defeated. After a day of waiting in battle formation, the Romans yielded to the night and rested, hopeful that there would be some kind of battle. The enemy, on the other hand, was extremely anxious and sent messengers to recall their raiding parties. Some returned, but those who were too far away didn't.

When dawn broke, the Romans left their camp, ready to attack the enemy's rampart if a fight didn't occur. After much of the day passed without any movement, Consul Valerius ordered the standards to be raised and they advanced. With the Roman battleline in motion coming toward them, the Aequians and the Volscians were ashamed that their victorious armies would now need to defend themselves with a rampart rather than their bravery and their weapons.

At their insistence, the Aequians and Volscians finally received a signal to attack from their generals. However, they weren't able to assemble fully. Half of them had left the gates, but the rest were trying to get to their positions. Valerius, before the enemy's battleline was firm, advanced to charge. The attack, delivered before the enemy were drawn together and sufficiently arranged, revealed little more than a mob of men, looking around in fear. The shouting and anger caused them to initially give ground; then, when they gathered and recovered their energy, their generals furiously rebuked them, asking whether they were going to yield to the same people they had already beaten. After this, they held their ground.

FREE SOLDIERS DEFEND FREE ROME

61. On the other side of the battle, Consul Valerius told the Romans to remember that they fight as free men for the first time in defense of a free Rome. They were conquering for themselves and not as spoils of

the decemvirs. The battle wasn't being led by Appius Claudius, but by Consul Valerius, a descendant of the liberators of the Roman people and a liberator, himself. He challenged them to prove that previous failures in battle were due to the failures of the generals as leaders, not the failures of soldiers. Let them show that it was disgraceful to show more courage in fighting against fellow citizens than against enemies, and to have been more fearful of slavery at home than abroad. No one's chastity had been in jeopardy except for Verginia's while at peace, and no citizen other than Appius Claudius had the power to pursue his dangerous lust. However, if the fortunes of war turned, the children of all would be in danger from so many thousands of the enemy. He didn't wish to imagine that either Jupiter or Mars, their father, would allow this to happen to the City founded under their auspices. He reminded them of the Aventine Hill and the Sacred Mount where freedom had been reestablished just a few months before. Return the original, successful leaders there and demonstrate that the Roman soldiers still had the same abilities after the decemvirs were expelled as they had before. Let them show that the courage of the Roman people hadn't diminished after the laws were equalized.

After speaking to the infantry, Valerius then turned to the cavalry and cried, "Come, young men! Show more bravery than the infantry, as you surpass them in honor and rank! At the first charge, the infantry will start the enemy running. Chase them and drive them out of the field with your cavalry. They won't withstand the attack and will hesitate rather than resist!"

The cavalry spurred their horses and charged toward the disordered enemy, already retreating from the infantry's attack. Breaking through their ranks, some rode on to the rear line, while others, circling around in open space, turned many fleeing men away from the camp, frightening them as they rode past. The line of infantry, along with the consul himself and the full force of the battle, advanced toward the camp, which, after a great slaughter, was taken with even greater plunder.

News of the battle reached the City and was met with a public celebration. The news of the battle also reached the Sabines as well as Consul Horatius' army, inspiring the soldiers to compete for similar glory.

HORATIUS' ARMY RISES

Consul Horatius had been training his army to do small skirmishes, helping them to rely on each other rather than dwelling on the shame they felt under the command of the decemvirs. These small battles had snowballed, building their confidence and hope. The Sabines ceaselessly provokes and challenges them, proud of their successes the previous year and questioning why they were wasting time with these small, petty skirmishes rather than engaging in a significant battle. Why not engage the enemy in a full battle line and give fortune a chance to decide the matter once and for all?

62. Consul Horatius' army had already built back a significant amount of courage, but they were angered at the thought that the other army under Consul Valerius would soon return to the City victorious over the Volscians and Aequians, while they, themselves, were being insulted and reviled by the Sabines' contemptuous behavior. When they would be able to defeat the enemy and if they could do it now?

When Consul Horatius learned the soldiers were feeling this way, he called a meeting. "I assume you have heard about the events in Algidum," he said, "The army behaved as an army of free people should. Thanks to Consul Valerius' wise leadership and the soldiers' bravery, we won. As for me, I'll act upon your feelings with the same great spirit and determination that you have shown me. We can either extend the war, which could be beneficial to us, or end it quickly. If we extend it, I'll ensure that your hopes and courage grow each day through the same training that I began with. If you feel courageous enough and want to resolve this now, let me hear your battle cry. This will show your willingness and bravery."

The soldiers enthusiastically shouted. Horatius acknowledged their decision, promising them that, with favor from the gods, he would act upon their wishes and lead them to the battlefield the next day. The soldiers spent the rest of the day preparing their weapons.

The following day, when the Sabines saw the Roman army lining up for battle, they also stepped forward, eager to fight. The battle was intense, as is expected between two confident armies. The Romans were inspired by their past victories, while the Sabines were encouraged by their recent successes.

CAVALRY, INFANTRY SHARE THE DANGER

The Sabines used a stratagem to strengthen their forces. They kept two-thousand men in reserve, outside their ranks, to attack the Romans' left wing during the battle. When the enemy almost surrounded and overpowered the Romans' left wing, a signal from the Romans' horn was heard, and six-hundred and forty Roman cavalry from two legions dismounted from their horses and pressed forward, rushing to the front. The cavalry not only stopped the enemy's progress, but also boosted the infantry's courage by sharing the danger with them. Seeing the cavalry getting off their horses to do the infantry's job made the infantry feel ashamed that the cavalry had to fight both on horseback and on foot, and that the infantry couldn't match the cavalry even when they were fighting without their horses.

63. The soldiers continued pushing forward into the battle with the Sabines, abandoning their previous position and reclaiming the territory they had lost. In an instant, not only was the fight back on, but one of the Sabine wings started to falter.

The cavalry, now protected by the infantry, returned to their horses. They then raced across to the other division to share their victory with their allies. At the same time, the cavalry attacked the enemy, who were losing hope due to the defeat of their stronger wing. No one showed more courage in that battle.

Consul Horatius was prepared for all situations; he praised the brave and scolded where the fight seemed to slow. When scolded, the army immediately showed the strength of brave men; and a sense of shame motivated them as much as praises encouraged the others. With a new battle cry and a united effort from all sides, the Romans pushed the enemy back; the Roman power could no longer be resisted.

The Sabines, chased in all directions through the country, left their possessions behind in their camp as spoils for the Romans. There the Romans recovered not just the allies' belongings, as at Algidum, but their own property, which had been lost due to the plundering of their lands.

SEEKING CREDIT (AND A TRIUMPH)

For this double victory, achieved in two battles and in two different places, the Senate begrudgingly decreed prayers in the name of the consuls for only a single day. In protest, the people went in large numbers to the temples on the second day to offer thanks. This second, unauthorized day of prayer was even more popular and eagerly attended by the people.

The consuls, by prior agreement, came to the City on the second day and summoned the Senate to the Campus Martius where they recounted all their victories performed. This was done while in front of the soldiers. Some prominent senators complained that the Senate being convened among the soldiers was done deliberately, and for no other reason than to intimidate them.

To avoid any basis for such an accusation, the consuls moved the Senate to the Flaminian Meadows, where the Temple of Apollo now stands. At that time, it was already referred to as the Temple of Apollo. There, with a large consensus from the senators, the triumph was denied.

Lucius Icilius, a plebeian tribune, took the issue to the plebeians. Many people came forward to argue against the measure, including Caius Claudius, who loudly stated that the consuls wished to triumph not over enemies but over the patricians. They were seeking a personal favor, he said, from the tribune in return for the favors they had given him, rather than celebrating a triumph for honor and virtue.

The decision of whether a triumph was deserved always lay with the Senate. Never before had it happened that a triumph was granted by the plebeians. Not even the kings had infringed upon the decision of this highest order. If the tribunes carried out all their powers in such a way that no public council was allowed to exist, the state would no longer be free, and laws wouldn't be equal if each order didn't maintain its own rights and its own dignity.

Much was said by the other senior senators which echoed the sentiment from Claudius, but all the tribes ultimately approved that proposal of a triumph. And, for the first time, a triumph was celebrated by order of the plebeians, without the authority of the Senate.

ELECTION INTEGRITY

64. A solid victory by the tribunes and the plebeians nearly developed into an unhealthy, indulgent abuse of power. A conspiracy was hatched among the tribunes to secure their re-election. To make the scheme less obvious, the tribunes also planned to extend the term of the consuls, arguing that the senators were trying to undermine the rights of the tribunes by disrespecting the consuls. However, the tribunes worried about the potential consequences. What if the consuls, before the laws were firmly established, were to challenge the new tribunes? They noted that not all consuls would be like Horatius and Valerius, who both put the plebeians' freedom before their own interests.

By fortunate chance, Marcus Duillius, an ex-tribune who understood the longer-term implications, was chosen by lot to oversee the elections. Since he foresaw public anger overflowing because of the tribunes' continued term, he declared he would accept no votes for them. His colleagues protested. They argued that the tribes should be able to vote for whomever they wanted. If they couldn't do this, Duillius should resign his role overseeing elections so that his colleagues could conduct the voting in accordance with the law rather than following the desires of the patricians.

Since controversy had broken out, Duillius sent for the consuls. He asked them about their plans for the consular elections, and they responded that they, themselves, would appoint new consuls. As they proceeded to the assembly, the consuls were asked if they would possibly accept re-election, considering their large contributions to the plebeians' liberty and military services. They didn't change their stance.

Marcus Duillius praised the consuls for their steadfastness and that they had persisted all the way to the end in not being like the decemvirs. He then held the election. Five tribunes were elected, but due to the aggressive campaigning of the nine tribunes, the other candidates couldn't secure enough tribal votes. Duillius dismissed the assembly and didn't hold a second one to fill the missing places. He had fulfilled the law, which only stated that the office of tribunes shouldn't be left vacant, but without specifying the number of tribunes.

Dullius suggested that the elected tribunes choose their colleagues. He recited the law's terms, which stated that if less than ten tribunes were elected, the tribunes may choose their colleagues, and those chosen would be legitimate tribunes. Duillius' colleagues tried to promote having more than ten tribunes, but he insisted that the republic couldn't have fifteen tribunes.

Then, having persevered until the end and thwarting his colleagues' ambitions of having fifteen tribunes, he resigned his office. This act earned the approval of both the patricians and the plebeians.

448 BC — THE CONSULS MAINTAIN PEACE

65. In the election of new tribunes, there was a clear intent to please the patricians. Two patricians, Spurius Tarpeius and Aulus Aternius, were elected as tribunes.

The newly elected consuls, Spurius Herminius Coritinesanus and Titus Verginius Caelimontanus, didn't strongly favor either the patricians or the plebeians. The consuls maintained peace both within and outside the City.

A tribune, Lucius Trebonius, was angry with the patricians. He felt that they had tricked him during the election of his colleagues. He proposed that whomever had started the voting process for the election of tribunes should continue until all ten tribunes were elected. He spent his time as a tribune causing trouble for the patricians, earning him the nickname Asper, meaning "cantankerous."

447 BC — LIBERTY VS. MODERATION

The next consuls, Marcus Geganius Macerinus and Caius Julius Iullus, managed to calm the conflict between tribunes and the young patricians without harshly opposing the tribunes and while maintaining the dignity of the senators. When a draft for the war against the Volscians and Aequians was announced, they kept the plebeians from rioting by telling them that all was peaceful both at home and abroad and that the draft wasn't needed. The consuls believed that the enemies were gaining courage due to the City's internal discord.

The preservation of peace was also of great concern. However, each group took advantage of the other's moderation. The young patricians began to mistreat the plebeians. When the tribunes tried to help the weaker party, they were initially unsuccessful. Later, the tribunes themselves were mistreated. This was especially true toward the end of the year when the power of the magistrates weakened. The plebeians began to long for tribunes like Lucius Icilius, feeling that the tribunes of the past two years had been ineffective. The older patricians, while thinking their young men were too aggressive, preferred this way instead of the plebeians being too powerful.

It's very difficult to balance liberty with moderation, as everyone wants to elevate themselves at the expense of others, pushing them down. While people try to protect themselves from fear, they cause others to fear them. When we defend ourselves from injury, we inflict injustices onto others, as if it were necessary in life to either commit injustices or suffer from them.

Chapter 15

FOR HEAVEN'S SAKE, WHAT DO YOU ALL WANT? (446 BC)

66. IN THE FOLLOWING year when Titus Quinctius Capitolinus Barbatus was elected consul for the fourth time, alongside Agrippa Furius Fusus, there were no immediate threats of war or internal conflict. However, both were on the horizon. The citizens' disagreements were escalating, with both the tribunes and the plebeians growing increasingly angry with the patricians. This tension was exacerbated whenever a trial date was set for a patrician, leading to further disputes in the assemblies.

Upon hearing reports of the first signs of discord, the Aequians and Volscians, as if given a signal, prepared for battle. Their leaders, eager for spoils, had convinced them that the Roman draft announced two years prior couldn't be enforced due to the plebeians' refusal to comply. They believed that no armies would be sent against them because military order was being undermined by lawlessness. Rome was no longer seen as its citizens' common, shared homeland. Instead, the hostility Rome had previously felt toward outsiders was now directed at each other. The Aequians and Volscians saw this as an opportunity to destroy those they viewed as wolves, blinded by their own internal strife.

After joining forces, the Aequians and the Volscians first attacked the Latin territory. When they encountered no resistance there, they moved closer to Rome itself, much to the delight of those who had advocated for the war. They carried out raids in the area around the Esquiline Gate, showing contempt for the City by devastating the fields nearby. They then retreated to Corbio without any opposition, taking their spoils with them.

"WHEN WILL OUR DISAGREEMENTS END?"

In response to this, Consul Quinctius called the plebeians to an assembly.

67. I understand that he expressed himself in this way:

"Even though I'm aware of no wrongdoing on my part, Romans, I've come here with immense shame. It's important for you to understand this. It should be recorded for future generations that the Aequians and Volscians, who were barely strong enough to fight our Hernician allies not long ago, have audaciously approached the walls of Rome, armed, during this fourth consulate of myself, Titus Quinctius."

"We have been living in such a way for a while now, given the situation, that positive news is a rarity these days. However, if I had known that such a giant disgrace was destined for this specific year, I'd have avoided this 'honor,' either by leaving the country in exile or by dying, if there were no other way. If the enemy which were at our gates had been armed, Rome could have been captured during my consulate. Truthfully, I've had enough honors. More than enough in life. I should have died during my third consulate."

"Whom do these cowardly enemies scorn? We, the consuls, or you, the citizens? If the fault lies with us, remove us from command as unworthy individuals. If that isn't enough, impose further punishment on us. But if the fault lies with you, may no god or man punish your offenses; you should only feel remorse for them. These enemies didn't scorn your cowardice, nor did they trust in their own bravery; having been defeated and chased away by you numerous times, stripped of their camp, deprived of their land, sent under the yoke, these enemies are familiar with both themselves and you."

"The anger and disagreement between the patricians and the plebeians have poisoned Rome and the disputes between the patricians and the plebeians have emboldened our enemies. The enemies see we have no limits in our pursuit of power, nor you plebeians in your pursuit of freedom. And while you're weary of patricians, and we're weary of plebeian magistrates, this fight has allowed our enemies to become stronger."

"For heaven's sake, what do you all want?"

"You yearned for tribunes, so we granted them for the sake of harmony."

"You desired decemvirs, so we allowed them to be appointed."

"You then grew tired of the decemvirs, so we forced them to resign."

"You remained angry at these same individuals when they became private citizens, so we allowed patrician men of the highest families and military rank to die or go into exile."

"You wanted to appoint tribunes again and you did so. Although we recognized that it was unfair to the patricians to appoint consuls in your favor, we have even seen a patrician magistracy conceded as a gift to the plebeians."

"We have endured, and we continue to endure the tribunes' aid, the right of the people to appeal, the decrees of the plebeians made binding on the patricians under the pretext of equalizing the laws, and the undermining of our privileges."

"When will our disagreements end? When will we be allowed to have a united City? When will we have one shared homeland? When defeated, we accept it with more grace than you do when victorious. Is it enough for us to fear you?"

"AGAINST US, YOU TAKE UP ARMS!"

"Against us the Aventine Hill was taken, the Sacred Mount was seized. The Esquiline Hill was almost captured by the enemy with the Volscians trying to climb the rampart, yet no one tried to dislodge them. Against us, you present yourselves as men! Against us, you take up arms!"

68. "You have stirred up trouble to the point where you have surrounded the Senate-house, turned the Forum into a battlefield, then filled the prison with the state's leading men. With that same fiery determination, you should march out through the Esquiline Gate, or if you're too scared to do that, just watch from the walls as your lands are destroyed by fire and sword! Watch the widespread looting! Watch as houses are set on fire with such intensity that there is smoke in every direction!"

"But you might say, the community is worse off because of these actions: the land is burned, the City is under siege, and all the glory of the war is with the enemy. What about your own personal interests? Soon, each of you will hear about your own private losses from the lands. What do you have at home to make up for these losses? Will the tribunes give you back what you have lost?"

"The tribunes will give you plenty of words, accusations against the leading men, laws upon laws, and public meetings. However, from being at these meetings, none of you has ever returned home richer or more fortunate. Has anyone ever brought back anything to his wife and children except hatred, disputes, and public and private quarrels, and from which, you have always been protected not by your own courage and honesty, but by the help of others."

"War Is Now at your Doorstep"

"But, by Hercules, when you were earning pay under us consuls, not under your tribunes or generals, in the camp, not in the Forum, the enemy trembled at your battle cry, not the Roman patricians in the assembly. You used to return home to your family and household gods in triumph after gaining spoils, taking land from the enemy, and amassing wealth and glory, both public and private. Now, instead, you let the enemy leave with your property. You stay tied to your assemblies. You live in the Forum. The need to go to war, which you avoid, still follows you around. It was a heavy burden for you to march against the Aequians and the Volscians before. Well, now the war is at your doorstep. If it isn't pushed back from here, it'll soon be within the City walls, and will climb the Citadel and Capitoline Hill, and then follow you into your very homes."

"Two years ago, the Senate ordered a draft to be held, and the army to march to Algidum. Yet we sit at home, bickering with each other like women and enjoying the present peace not understanding that, after this brief peaceful break, complex wars are sure to return."

"I know there are many more pleasant topics than this one, but even if I didn't need to speak about it, I speak from necessity. Necessity forces me to speak the truth rather than what is convenient and pleasant. I'd indeed like to please you, Romans, but I'm much more concerned that you should be safe, no matter what you think of me. It's a fact of life that the person who speaks to a crowd for his own benefit is more popular than the one who only has the public good in mind."

"That is, unless perhaps you think that those public flatterers, those plebeian agitators who neither let you go to war nor live in peace, stir you up for your own cause. Because when you're stirred up, you're a source of notoriety and profit for them. These flatterers see that they aren't important to either side when the two different sides are in harmony, so they prefer to lead a bad cause rather than no cause at all."

"f you're finally tired of this, and if you're willing to return to the ways of your ancestors, and of yourselves in the past, I'm willing to accept any punishment if I don't defeat, drive away, and strip their camps for spoils, those enemies who are ravaging our lands, and transfer this fear of war, which is now causing you so much alarm, from our gates and walls to their cities."

Uniting Rome for War

69. Rarely has the speech of a popular tribune been better received by the plebeians than this speech, given by the strictest of consuls. The young men of military age, who usually used refusal-to-enlist as a weapon against the patricians during crises, began to look forward to going to war. The plight of the rural plebeians, their land being plundered and the wounded, who brought reports worse than that which could be seen by the eyes, brought a sense of rage and revenge to the entire City.

When the Senate gathered, they all looked to Consul Quinctius as the sole defender of Roman majesty. The leading senators declared that his speech was worthy of his consular command, worthy of his many previous consulships, worthy of his life full of honors, and that, as much as he received these honors, he deserved them more often. Previous consuls had either tried to please the plebeians by betraying the dignity of the patricians or had made the plebeians more rebellious by harshly defending the rights of the patricians. However, Titus Quinctius gave a speech that respected the dignity of the Senate and promoted harmony among the different classes and was appropriate for the times.

They urged Consul Quinctius and Consul Furius to protect the interests of the state. The tribunes should unite with the consuls to keep the war away from the City and its walls, and to persuade the plebeians to obey the Senate in this dangerous situation. They asked that the tribunes assist the plebeian citizens whose City was almost besieged and the lands were destroyed.

Everyone agreed that a draft was necessary, and it was held. When the consuls announced that there was no time to consider excuses and that all men liable for service should report to the Campus Martius at dawn the next day. They would grant time after the war was completed to hear any reasons why anyone chose to not enlist. For those whose excuses weren't legitimate, they would be considered deserters and treated as such. The next day, the entire youth showed up.

Each group of one hundred chose their own centurions, and two senators were put in charge of each cohort, about four-hundred eighty soldiers. We have heard that all these steps were taken so quickly that the army led by the standards quickly brought onto the field by the quaestors from the treasury. They started to move from the Campus Martius at the fourth hour [nine to ten] that morning and stopped at the tenth milestone to set up camp. The army was followed by a few cohorts of experienced soldiers who volunteered to join.

The next day, the Romans saw the enemy, and they set up camp near their other camp at Corbio.

On the third day, the Romans, driven by anger, and the enemy, driven by guilt and despair, didn't hesitate to start fighting.

70. In the Roman army, the two consuls had equal power. However, Consul Furius willingly gave up his supreme command to Consul Quinctius. This was beneficial in handling important matters, as Consul Quinctius responded with respect at Consul Furius' humility. He shared all his plans and honors with Furius, treating him as an equal even though he was no longer one.

In the battle line, Quinctius led the right wing and Furius the left wing. The central line was given to Spurius Postumius Albus, the lieutenant general. Publius Sulpicius, the other lieutenant-general, was put in charge of the cavalry. The infantry fought extremely well from the right wing, resisting the Volscians with great bravery.

VICTORY OVER MEN (AND HORSES)

Publius Sulpicius led his cavalry through the enemy's center. He could have returned to the Roman side before the enemy could regroup, but it seemed better to attack the enemy's rear and scatter them with a two-fold attack. However, the Volscian and Aequian cavalry intercepted them and engaged them in battle, thus keeping Sulpicius from moving forward.

Sulpicius shouted to his men that there was no time to delay; they were surrounded and cut off from the Roman army unless the cavalry fought with all their strength. It wasn't enough merely to drive away the enemy's cavalry; they must finish off both the horses and the men so that neither could return to the battle and fight again. The densely packed enemy infantry would give way to the cavalry, which wouldn't be able to put up any resistance. His men listened and, with a single rush, they routed the entire enemy cavalry, threw many men from their horses, and stabbed the men and their horses with javelins. This ended the battle with the cavalry.

Sulpicius' cavalry then ran through the enemy's infantry line, sending messengers to report their actions to the consuls including where the enemy line was already faltering. The news encouraged the Romans and discouraged the Aequians who were retreating. It was in the center that the Aequians began to lose, as the cavalry broke their ranks. Then, at that point, the Aequians' left wing started to lose under Consul Quinctius' leadership.

The right side was the most challenging. Consul Furius, youthful, lively, and bold, felt that every part of the battle was going better than his. He seized some of the standards from the standard-bearers and, advancing, began to hurl them into the crowded enemy. The Roman soldiers, fearing disgrace, attacked the enemy, and victory was achieved on all fronts.

At that time, Consul Quinctius sent a messenger to report that he was victorious and was ready to storm the enemy's camp. He didn't want to do it until he knew that Consul Furius had also won on the left wing; he wanted him to bring his men with him so that the entire army could claim the spoils. Accordingly, Furius joined his victorious colleague at the front of the enemy's camp. Both consuls easily defeated the few defenders and took the fortifications without a struggle. They returned with a vast amount of spoils, including their own possessions that had been lost during the devastation of the lands.

It's unclear whether Consuls Quinctius and Furius asked for a triumph or if the Senate awarded them one. There is no reason given for this honor being overlooked or not expected. It's possible that after a triumph was denied to Consuls Horatius and Valerius, who had ended the Sabine war in addition to fighting the Aequians and Volscians, the consuls were too embarrassed to ask for a triumph for only half of their services. The consuls may have feared that if they did receive it, it would seem to be based on favoritism rather than merit.

THE PLEBEIANS STEAL FROM THE ALLIES

71. The honorable victory the consuls had won over their enemies was soon tarnished by a shameful decision by the plebeians about their allies' borders. The states of Aricia and Ardea, who had often fought over a disputed piece of land, were tired from their many losses. Both states chose the Roman plebeians to decide who the land belonged to.

When they came to present their cases, a public meeting was arranged by the officials. A heated debate followed the meeting. However, when it was time for the tribes to be called and the plebeians to vote, an elderly plebeian named Publius Scaptius stood up and said, "Consuls, if I may speak, I'll not let the plebeians be misled in this matter." Although the consuls shouted that he shouldn't be heard, claiming he was speaking vainly ordering the public matter be removed, Scaptius appealed to the tribunes.

The tribunes, who usually follow the crowd rather than lead it, allowed Publius Scaptius to speak because the plebeians wanted to hear him.

Scaptius began by stating that he was eighty-three years old and he had served in the disputed area during his twentieth military campaign when war was being fought at Corioli. It had been forgotten over time but was still clear in his memory: the disputed land had belonged to Corioli, and after Corioli was captured, it became the public property of the Roman plebeians by right of war. He was surprised that Ardea and Aricia thought they could take the land from the Roman plebeians, who they have now made the decision-makers, even though the plebeians had never claimed the land while Corioli was still standing.

He felt that he didn't have much time left to live, but he couldn't stop himself to allow the land, which he had helped to win as a soldier, be taken without protest using the only means he had left: his voice. He strongly advised the plebeians not to harm their own interests through useless shame.

72. The consuls were shocked when they realized that Scaptius wasn't only being heard in silence but also with approval. A terrible and shameful act was taking place with both gods and men as witnesses.

They called for the leaders of the Senate and together they approached the various tribes, urging them to not commit a terrible crime by turning the judges' proceedings into a dispute for their own personal gain. Even if a judge could legally protect his own property, no amount of land acquired could compensate for the harm done by alienating their allies through unfairness. The damage to their reputation and the loss of trust would be far more significant, almost incalculable. To have this reported by ambassadors, to have it publicized, to have allies hear it, and enemies too? What sadness it would give allies! What joy it would give enemies! Would neighboring states blame this action on Scaptius, a notorious chatterbox at meetings? It would make Scaptius famous enough to have it inscribed below his portrait, but it would paint the Roman plebeians as tyrants and obstructors of others' rights. Would any judge in a private case ever behave this way, awarding himself the disputed property? We doubt that Scaptius himself would do such a thing, despite his apparent lack of shame.

The consuls and the senators cried out these things, but Scaptius' greed and the influence of that greed were more powerful. The tribes, having been called, judged that the disputed land was the public property of the Roman plebeians.

It isn't disputed that the verdict would have been the same if they had sought other judges. However, the excellence of the cause didn't, not even a little, justify or make the disgrace of the judgment forgivable. This was seen as more disgraceful and harsher to the Roman senators than to the Aricians and Ardeans.

The rest of the year passed without any City or foreign disturbances.

DICTIONARY

AEDILE – THE POSITION of aedile was an elected office of the plebeians. Two aediles were responsible for maintenance of public buildings, the running of public festivals, games, and the supply of food in the marketplace. They also were responsible for public order. See Curule Aedile for the position changing.

AES RUDE – Sometimes called "assis, as, asses, or ass". Irregularly shaped pieces of bronze known as aes rude (*rough bronze*) which needed to be weighed for each transaction. The bronze nuggets usually weighed 5 pounds each. As an example: fines or bail at a surety of 3,000 aes rude would be 15,000 pounds. Ten sureties would be 150,000 pounds.

AGRARIAN LAW - (Latin *ager*, meaning "land") There existed two kinds of land in ancient Rome: private and public land (*ager publicus*), which included common pasture. There were various attempts by the plebeians to regulate the laws of public land distribution. This struggle was ongoing for many years between the patricians and the plebeians which was known as the Conflict of Orders.

ANCILIA - (sing. ancile) The original ancile was said to have fallen from the skies in the time of Numa. In order to protect it from damage or robbery, Numa had 11 shields made just like it to disguise the original. The shape of the shield was unusual in that it was shaped like an oval but the sides were indented in a long curve. These twelve shields, "ancilia", were kept in the Temple of Mars Gradivus and on the kalends of March (March 1st) they were taken out to celebrate a feast to Mars Gradivus. The feast lasted several days with the twelve Salii, or priests of Mars, carrying the sacred shields about the city, singing songs in praise of Mars Gradivus, Numa, and Mamurius Veturius, who created the eleven copies. While performing a dance, the twelve Salii sang and they struck the shield with rods, emphasizing the rhythm of the song.

ARUSPEX - (aruspices, sing.) In ancient Rome, a priest who practiced the foretelling of events, especially by examining the internal organs of animals.

ATELLAN FARCE - (aka Oscan Games) Masked impromptu rustic plays of country life and adopted for intermissions and after plays during the Republic and up to the time of Tiberius. The stock characters' masks were generally grotesque.

AUGUR - One of the members of a religious college whose job was to watch for and interpret the activities of birds. These signs (auspices) could be positive or negative and were sent by the gods as a comment on any proposed undertaking. Auspex, another word for augur, can be translated to "one who looks at birds".

AUSPICES - (Latin auspicium) Which means "looking at birds". Depending upon the birds, the auspices from the gods could be positive or negative (auspicious or inauspicious). The augurs job was to read the flights of birds to determine the will of the Gods. The auspices showed the Romans that it may or may not be a good thing they were about to do. There was no explanation for the decision, just that it was the will of the gods.

AUSPEX – See **AUGUR**

BEADLE – A beadle is an official who may usher, keep order, make reports, and assist in religious functions; or a minor official who carries out various civil, educational or ceremonial duties of a household. Beadles also had the responsibility of maintaining discipline during the observance of public worship.

BUCKLER – The buckler was a small shield that usually fit on the wrist or forearm of the soldier and was used by the cavalry or in hand-to-hand combat.

CAESO QUINCTIUS - Caeso Quinctius L. f. L. n. Cincinnatus was the son of the Dictator. During the political struggles between the patricians and the plebeians Caeso took the side of the patricians and, though having no position of power or title, he and his followers prevented the plebeian tribunes and plebeians from meeting in the Forum and conducting their business. They did this by using violence to drive away the plebeians. His trial for obstructing the plebeian tribunes in 461 BC was one of the key events in the Conflict of Orders in the years that led up to the decemvirate.

CENSOR - A censor was one of two senior magistrates in the city of ancient Rome who supervised public morals, maintained the census, and supervised tax obligations. The job was given to former consuls and lasted up to 18 months.

CINCINNATUS - Lucius Quinctius Cincinnatus was a Roman patrician of the Quinctius family who was a statesman and military leader of the early Roman Republic who became a legendary figure of Roman virtue—particularly civic virtue—by the time of the late Republic.

CIRCUMVALLATION - The military process of surrounding an enemy fort with armed forces to prevent entry or escape. It serves both to cut communications with the outside world and to prevent supplies and reinforcements from being introduced.

CITADEL - The citadel was a fortified hill that is often located within a city or town on which several temples were built. Often there was a fortified structure designed to protect the citizens against enemies.

CIVIC CROWN - A wreath of oak leaves woven to form a crown. It was awarded to Roman citizens who saved the life of a fellow citizen being threatened by an enemy usually in or near the City. The citizen saved must attest to it and no one else was a witness.

CLIENT - In Rome a client was a free man who entrusted himself to another and received protection in return. A client was a bonafide position, hereditary, and recognized by law although not defined or enforced. The law was more rigid in the case of the freedman (freed slave), who was automatically a client of his former owner. Ordinary clients supported their patron in political and private life and accompanied him when he went out. The size of a man's group of clients, their wealth and status, added to his prestige, popularity, and political power. In exchange, clients received benefits of various kinds, such as food or money and help in the courts.

COHORT – A legionary cohort of the early republic consisted of six *centuriae*, or centuries, each consisting of 80 legionaries, for a total of 480 men.

COLLEGE OF PONTIFFS - The College of Pontiffs (Collegium Pontificum) were the highest-ranking priests of the state religion. The members of the college were the Pontifex Maximus and the other pontifices, the rex sacrorum, the 15 flamens, and the Vestal Virgins.

COLLEGIUM - A collegium (pl.: collegia) or college was any group in ancient Rome that acted as a legal entity. They could be civil or religious. The word "collegium" literally means "society". They functioned as social clubs or religious groups sharing the same variety of interests such as: politics, religion, different professions, civic duties or trade activities. These associations helped the members' influence on politics and the economy and encouraged them to act as lobbying groups and representatives for traders and merchants.

COMITIA CURIATA - Composed of 30 curiae, or local groups, drawn from three ancient tribes, assembly of these curiae, the Comitia Curiata, was for a time the sole legal representative of the entire Roman people. The Comitia Curiata dates from the time of the Roman kings. During the Republic it was a general assembly but only patricians could vote. It was here that the military tribunes, consuls, consular tribunes, praetors, etc. were elected.

COMITA TRIBUTA - This was an assembly consisting of all Roman plebeians organized by tribes and it excluded patricians. It was convened to make decisions on legislative or judicial matters, or to hold elections. Patricians felt they were not bound by these laws as they were not included. This changed later on.

COMITIUM - The Comitium was the original open-air public meeting space of ancient Rome. The Comitium was in front of the meeting house of the Roman Senate – the Curia Hostilia. It was the meeting place of the Curiate Assembly, the earliest popular assembly of organized voting divisions of the Republic. Later, during the Roman Republic, the Tribal Assembly and the Plebeian Assembly met there.

CONFLICT OF THE ORDERS – also Struggle of the Orders, was a political struggle between the plebeians (commoners) and patricians (aristocrats) of the ancient Roman Republic lasting from 500 BC to 287 BC in which the plebeians sought political equality with the patricians.

CONSUL – A consul was the highest elected public official of the Roman Republic (c. 509 BC to 27 BC). Normally two were elected to lead for one year. The consul was the second highest position in power below that of the censor held by previous consuls.

CONSULARS AND CONSULAR RANK – Former consuls were often called upon to fill in when additional help was needed. Sometimes former consuls were assigned new duties (e.g., guarding Rome while the current consuls were away at battle). The Romans were smart in utilizing former consuls, because these men had the experience and expertise to handle critical jobs. Another former consul role was that of pro consul which was an extension of the consul's year to act as a representative of the new consul, usually in battles and for no more than 6 months.

CONSULAR TRIBUNES – Military tribunes with consular power were created during the Conflict of the Orders, along with the position of the censor, in order to give the plebeian order access to higher levels of government without having to reform the office of consul; plebeians could be elected to the office of consular tribune. The consular tribunes often replaced the consuls as the leaders. The consular tribunes not only handled the military affairs of Rome, but also the administrative needs of the City as well.

CO-OPT - Appointing an individual to membership of a committee or other body by invitation of the existing members. The passage of *Lex Trebonia* forbade the co-opting of colleagues to fill vacant positions of tribunes. Its purpose was to prevent the patricians from pressuring the tribunes to appoint colleagues sympathetic to or chosen from the aristocracy.

CURIA - (plural **curiae**) Curia has two meanings. It can be a building or meeting place for the Senate to meet in, or it can mean a political division of the people.

CURIA HOSTILIA - Built by King Tullus Hostilius. After the overthrow of the monarchy in 509 BC, the Curia Hostilia became the main meeting place for the Roman Republic Senate, and was perhaps the single most important building in Roman politics. While the Curia Hostilia was the main meeting place for the Senate, it was not the only place the Senate could meet.

CURIO - The curia was presided over by a curio (pl.: curiones), who was always at least 50 years old, and was elected for life. The curio undertook the religious affairs of the curia. He was assisted by another priest, known as the flamen curialis.

CURULE AEDILE - The curule aediles were the magistrates originally chosen from the patricians, however it then changed to alternating years. Responsible for the care and supervision of the markets and they also issued edicts, mainly rules as to buying and selling, and contracts for bargain and sale. They could also act as judges. The privileges of the curule aediles included a fringed toga, a curule chair, and the right to ancestral masks.

CURULE CHAIR – A style of chair reserved in ancient Rome for the use of the highest government dignitaries and usually made like a foldable, backless stool with curved legs. Often inlaid with ivory, with or without arms, it was a sign of power and was bestowed on such officials as the dictator, master of the horse, censor, consul, praetor, interrex, curule aedile, and later, the emperor.

DECEMVIRS – A special commission of ten members who ruled in place of consuls in ancient Rome circa 451-450 BC. Their primary purpose was to draw up Rome's first code of law, The Laws of the Twelve Tables. Because of their abuse of power, it was abandoned after two years.

DICTATOR – The dictator was the highest official in the Roman Republic that was appointed in an emergency. Usually, a dictator was appointed to conduct military campaigns and to quell civil unrest. The dictator was given full power in the pursuit of his cause and his authority was nearly absolute. However, he could only pursue the task for which he was appointed. As soon as the task was completed the dictator must resign.

DUUMVIR – (duumviri plural) A magistracy of two men who were assigned specific jobs. Early on they had charge of the Sibylline Books which they referred to in dangerous times to see what the gods demanded for the sins of the people. Later they could be judges or they could be assigned to administer the sacred rites or deal with public finance or run elections in the comitium.

EQUITES - The *equites* ('horse' or 'cavalrymen', though sometimes referred to as "knights" in English), made up of patricians in the early Roman Republic, constituted the second of the property-based classes of ancient Rome, ranking below the senatorial class. A member of the equestrian order was known as an *eques*.

EXODIA - Humorous verses often performed between serious plays by young patrician males only, who were not looked down on.

FASCES - A bundle of wooden rods with a projecting blade bound together by leather thongs and carried by a *lictor* (bodyguard) in ancient Rome as a symbol of a magistrate's power. Fasces represented that a man held authority.

FASTI – Ancient Roman *fasti* were calendars that recorded religious observances and officially commemorated events. They were usually displayed at a prominent public location such as a major temple.

FETIAL – A type of priest in ancient Rome. They formed a collegium devoted to Jupiter as the patron of good faith. The duties of the fetials included advising the Senate on foreign affairs and international treaties. They were sent to foreign states making formal proclamations of peace or war. They were also used to confirm treaties with foreign states.

FLAMEN - (pl: flamines) A priest assigned to the worship of one deity only. There were 15 *flamines*. The most important were Dialis, Martialis, and Quirinalis, who represented Jupiter, Mars, and Quirinus, respectively. A flamen was picked from the patrician class and led by the *Pontifex Maximus*. They had a distinctive dress, its most notable feature being the *apex*, a conical cap. They held daily sacrifices, and they were subject to strict rules and taboos. Their wives, the *flaminicae*, were their helpers and were also subject to the same rules.

FORMER CONSUL - A prior consul who is called upon for various duties. They tend to be left behind to manage the City.

GABINE CINCTURE - The *cinctus Gabinus* was a way of wearing the toga and thought to have originated in the town of Gabii. It was also later claimed to have been part of the Etruscan priests' clothing. The cincture allowed free use of both arms, particularly when worn during combat and later in some religious rituals, particularly those involving use of the toga to cover the head (capite velato).

GREAT GAMES – There were two kinds of Roman games: sacred or religious games and games of physical prowess. At first the games of the early Roman Republic had religious significance, thanking the gods for help during a battle. Then later the 'secular' games were purely for entertainment, some lasting two weeks.

GUARDIAN – In ancient Rome, all women were under an adult male guardian. That guardian was the oldest male in the household be it a father, grandfather, husband, uncle, or even oldest male child. The wife of the guardian was responsible for taking care of the home and family.

HASTATI - The newer or inexperienced foot soldiers who were the first line of defense armed with spears or javelins.

HISTRIONES - Dancers with mimic gestures to the music of a flute. Introduced by Etruscans who were hired to perform. Later non-citizens, freed-men, strangers or slaves learned the dance to perform. They were looked down upon and not allowed to be citizens or serve as soldiers.

ICILIAN LAW - By the *Icilian Law* the land on the Aventine Hill was deemed to be public land and divided into plots for the plebeians. The patricians were compensated for the value of their buildings already there. It was considered important for the independence of the plebeians that the patricians should not be their landlords, and thus able to control their votes.

IDES - For the months of March, May, July and October, the Ides fell on the 15th day. In every other month, the Ides fell on the 13th day. The third day of the Ides of August refers to August 15th which is the third day of a yearly celebration.

INTERNATIONAL LAW - **Jus Gentium** - Law of Nations. Early international law was religion-based and was about the concept of the "just war" (*bellum justum*), which could only be declared with a ritual by the fetial priests before any fighting could occur. Foreign ambassadors were protected by the *ius gentium*, and it was not only a religious violation to harm an envoy but the violation of international law.

INTERREGES see **INTERREX**

INTERREX – (pl: **interreges**) Initially, the interrex was appointed after the death of the king of Rome until the election of his successor, hence its name – a ruler "between kings" (Latin *inter reges*). The interrex position was retained during the Roman Republic when both consuls or consular tribunes were unable to assume their duties, usually due to elections being blocked. An interrex ruled for only five days, and sometimes many in a row would be appointed when there was no decision, the record being fifteen interreges in 326 BC. Chosen from among the senators, the position was often used to stop the plebeians from reaching power or passing laws during the Conflict of Orders.

INTERREGNUM – (pl: interregna) A period when normal government is suspended, especially between successive reigns.

JUGERA – A jugera was a Roman unit of area, equivalent to a rectangle 240 Roman feet in length and 120 feet in width (0.623 acre). The *jugerum* contained 28,800 square feet, while the English acre contains 43,560.

LECTISTERNIUM - A supplication ceremony, consisting of a meal offered to gods and goddesses spread on couches. The ceremony took place "for the first time" in Rome in the year 399 BC, after a plague had caused the Sibylline Books to be consulted by the duumviri sacris faciundis, the two priestly officials who maintained the archive. Again in 347 BC ten men were sent to check the Sibylline Books during another plague. Three couches were prepared for three pairs of gods – Apollo and Latona – Hercules and Diana – Mercury and Neptune. The feast lasted for eight (or seven) days, and was also celebrated by private individuals. The citizens kept an open house, quarrels were forgotten, debtors and prisoners were released, and everything was done to banish sorrow.

LEX CANULEIA – The Lex Canuleia, established in 445 B.C. in ancient Rome, permitted plebeians to marry patricians, promoting equality between the social classes and advancing towards a more just and fair society. Five years earlier, as part of the process of establishing the Twelve Tables of Roman law, the second decemvirate had placed severe restrictions on the plebeian order, including a prohibition on the intermarriage of patricians and plebeians.

LEX PUBLILIA - This law allowed plebeians to vote for their own plebeian tribunes in their own assembly, held in the Comita Tributa, instead of it being supervised and influenced by patricians.

LEX SACRATA – Not technically a law, this was an oath sworn by the plebeians to protect the plebeian tribunes and to punish with death anyone who should harm the holders of this office. Also, at times of military emergency, the compulsorily drafted soldiers swore to follow their commanders to the death.

LEX TRABONIA - See **TREBONIAN LAW**

LIBRI LINTEI - See **LINEN BOOKS**

LICTOR - A public officer, who were bodyguards for the chief Roman magistrates. A lictor was strong, capable of physical work. They were exempted from military service, received a salary, and were organized in a group. Often, they were personally chosen by the magistrate they were supposed to serve. The lictors had to inflict punishment on those who were condemned by the magistrates. Originally, lictors were chosen from the plebeians, but later they seemed to have been freedmen. They carried wooden rods held together with leather surrounding axes that symbolized the power to carry out capital punishment. They followed the magistrate wherever he went, including the Forum, his house, temples, and the baths.

LINEN BOOKS – The *libri lintei*, also known as the "linen rolls," were a collection of Etruscan books in ancient Rome written on linen, possibly from notes taken on linen clothing. All have been lost except a single Etruscan Liber Linteus, because it had been used as a mummy wrapping. The only way we know of them is from references by Roman authors who refer to them in their writings of history or mythology.

LUSTRUM - The lustrum was originally a sacrifice for making amends and purification offered by one of the censors in the Campus

Martius after the taking of the census was over. The sacrifice was often in the form of an animal sacrifice, known as a suovetaurilia. These censuses were taken at five-year intervals, thus a *lŭstrum* came to refer to the five-year inter-census period.

MAGISTER EQUITUM - See **MASTER OF THE HORSE**

MANTLET - In ancient times, the Mantlet was typically constructed of natural materials and wood. It would form a defensive wall or shield that soldiers could use as a cover from arrows.

MASTER OF THE HORSE – The Master of the Horse (Latin: Magister Equitum) in the Roman Republic was a position appointed and dismissed by the Roman dictator, and expired when the dictator resigned, typically a term of six months. He served as the dictator's main lieutenant. In the dictator's absence, the Magister Equitum stepped in as his representative, and exercised the same powers as the dictator. It was usually necessary for the Magister Equitum to have already held the office of praetor. Therefore, the Magister Equitum was entitled to the insignia of a praetor, the toga praetexta and an escort of six lictors.

MILITARY TRIBUNES WITH CONSULAR AUTHORITY – See **CONSULAR TRIBUNES**

MURAL CROWN - A crown which represents city walls, towers, or fortresses awarded to a soldier who first climbed the wall of a besieged city or fortress and successfully places the flag representing his army upon it.

NEW MAN - (Novus homo) The first of his family to attain consul status. The term was used with scorn to belittle the newcomer as the patricians tried to keep themselves exclusive. Becoming a consul automatically made you a senator, however as the new man you were not treated well. This would change in time.

OVATION - A general who did not earn a triumph might be granted an *ovatio,* in which he walked or rode on horseback, wearing the purple-bordered toga of an ordinary magistrate and a wreath of myrtle.

PALISADES - Palisade derives from the Latin word *"palus"*, meaning "stake", specifically when used side by side to create a wooded defensive wall. Roman soldiers usually carried 3 or 4 long stakes which were used in multiple ways.

PLEBEIAN TRIBUNES – These tribunes could advocate and propose legislation on behalf of the plebeians, and veto the actions of the magistrates or other officials. See Tribunes of the People.

POMERIUM - The pomerium was originally an area of ground on both sides of the city walls. Livy states that it was an Etruscan tradition to consecrate this area by augury and that it was technically unlawful to inhabit or to farm the area of the pomerium, which in part had the purpose of preventing buildings from being erected close to the wall.

PONTIFEX MAXIMUS – The Pontifex Maximus was chief high priest of the College of Pontiffs.. He did not serve for a fixed period but for life, and he remained, officially, a citizen. They were responsible for the Roman state religion as a whole and for several religious positions such as the augures, the decemviri sacris faciundis and the fetiales. Because the Pontifex Maximus was not a real magistrate, he was not allowed to wear the toga with the purple border. The Pontifex Maximus was also responsible for the eighteen priestesses of the goddess Vesta (Vestal Virgins).

PONTIFF – The pontiffs, (pontifices), or priests, cared for sacred matters which were ceremonies relating to the worship of the gods, especially sacrifice and prayer and about the proper addressing of people to gods and people to people, when divine matters were also important.

PORTA PRINCIPALIS – One of the main side gates into a legions' camp.

PRAEROGATIVE CENTURIES - The *praerogatives* were the eighteen centuries of knights, which voted first; if they agreed, the other centuries were not called.

PRAETEXTA - A toga with a broad purple border worn by certain magistrates and priests and by young boys until they assumed the toga virilis when reaching manhood.

PRAETOR – Magistrates ranking below consul. A man acting in one of two official capacities: the commander of an army, and as an elected magistrate who had the role of a judge. They often exercised extensive authority in the government in the absence of consuls. A man had to serve as praetor before being elected as a consul.

PRIMUS PILUS - The highest ranking centurion of the first cohort of a Roman legion. He was a career soldier and an experienced advisor to the legate (his boss).

PRINCIPES - The second line of foot soldiers after the *hastati* who were more experienced and fought with sword and shield.

PRO CONSUL - In the ancient Roman Republic, a pro consul was a consul whose powers had been extended for a specific period after his regular term of one year, often as a representative of the current consul and usually as a general in a battle.

PRODIGY - Phenomenon, portent, wonder, prognostication, prophecy. They are signs of nature in the form of lightning, earthquakes, apparitions of light or fire, volcanic eruptions, plagues of locusts, a rain of stones or blood, sweating or bleeding statues of gods, but also monstrosities among humans and animals and more.

PUBLICOLA - See **VALERIUS**

QUAESTOR – An elected official who supervised the state treasury and conducted audits. When assigned to provincial governors, the duties were mainly administrative and logistical, but also could expand to encompass military leadership and command.

RAMPART - The first step in a Roman siege was usually to surround the city by building a wall (rampart) or series of fortifications, cutting off all supplies and reinforcements to the defenders. This allowed the Romans to isolate the city and deprive the defenders of food, water, and other essentials.

ROSTRA – The Rostra was a large platform built in the city of Rome that stood during the republican and imperial periods. Speakers would stand on the rostra and face the north side of the Comitium towards the senate house and deliver orations to those assembled in between.

RUFULI - There are two kinds of military tribunes, the first consisting of those called *Rufuli* which are ordinarily appointed in the army; the second are the *comitiati*, who are designated at the Comitia Centuriata in Rome from which the Consuls and Consular Tribunes, Praetors, etc. are elected.

SACRED LAW - See **LEX SACRATA**

SALII -(Latin: "Dancers") A priesthood usually associated with the worship of Mars, the god of war. The twelve *Salii* were patrician youths who used song and dance as part of religious ritual. They were dressed as warriors with an embroidered tunic, a breastplate, a short red cloak, a sword, and a spiked headdress. They were given twelve bronze shields called *ancilia*, which resembled a figure eight. One of the shields was said to have fallen from heaven in the reign of King Numa and eleven copies were made to protect the identity of the sacred shield. It was prophesied that as long as the shield is safe so would the Roman people be safe. The Salii are sometimes credited with the opening and closing of the war cycle which would last from March to October.

SIBYLLINE BOOKS - The Sibylline Books were a collection of Greek rhymed verses that, according to tradition, were purchased from a sibyl by the last king of Rome, Lucius Tarquinius Superbus, and were consulted in moments of crises through the history of the Roman Republic and the Empire.

SOLON - In 594 BC in Greece, Solon was a ruler who instituted reforms to help Athenian society. Athenian citizens had the right to participate in assembly meetings. He started a wider range of property classes rather than just the aristocracy. His constitutional reforms included establishing four property classes. The classifications were based on how much money a man's estate made per year. This allowed every free citizen of Athens who owned property to have some influence in government. Under these reforms, the boule (a council of 400 members, with 100 citizens from each of Athens' four tribes) ran daily affairs and set the political agenda. Another major contribution to democracy was Solon's setting up an Assembly, which was open to all the male citizens. Solon also made significant economic reforms including canceling existing debts, freeing debtors, and no longer allowing borrowing on the security of one's own person as a means of restructuring enslavement and debt in Athenian society.

SPOLIA OPIMA – The spolia opima were the armor, arms, and other effects that an ancient Roman general stripped from the body of an opposing general he killed in hand-to-hand combat which was then brought back to Rome and dedicated at the temple of Jupiter Feretrius on the Capitoline Hill. Aulus Cornelius Cossus was a Roman general in the early Republic who is famous for being the second (secunda) Roman, after Romulus (prima), to be awarded the spolia opima, Rome's highest military honor.

SURETY - (Sureties, plural) - Essentially a bond. A surety is an entity or an individual who assumes the duty of paying the debt in the event that a debtor fails or is not able to make the payments. The bronze nuggets, **a**es rude, usually weighed 5 pounds each. In the case of Caeso, each surety at 3,000 aes rude would be 15,000 pounds. Ten sureties would be 150,000 pounds.

SUTLER - A person who followed an army and sold provisions to the soldiers. The traditional sutler followed troops and sold them supplies at hugely inflated prices.

TERENTILLIAN LAW - Proposed by Caius Terentillius Arsa in 462 BC that five men be chosen to write down the laws establishing consular power. The senate disagreed. After much squabbling over many years three men were sent to Athens to learn the laws and customs and to return with information. By 448 BC the Law of Twelve Tables was established by the ten decemvirs who were charged with creating it.

TESTUDO - (plural Testudines) The testudo or tortoise formation was a type of shield-wall formation commonly used by the Roman legions during battles, particularly sieges. Used for protection against attacks from above, consisting either of a movable arched structure or of overlapping shields held by the soldiers over their heads.

TOGA PRAETEXTA – Adopted by the Romans from the Etruscans. It was a white toga with a broad purple stripe on its border, worn over a tunic with two broad, vertical purple stripes. It was a formal costume for curule magistrates in their official functions, and traditionally, the Kings of Rome.

TORQUE - A necklace ring worn by both men and women. It was made of rigid metal and often the metal was twisted. It usually had an ornamental opening in the front.

TREBONIAN LAW - The Lex Trebonia was a law passed in 448 BC to forbid the plebeian tribunes from co-opting colleagues to fill vacant positions. Its purpose was to prevent the patricians from pressuring the plebeian tribunes to appoint colleagues sympathetic to or chosen from the patricians.

TRIARII – The triarii were the oldest and wealthiest soldiers, usually in their thirties, and in battle they stood as the third line of defense behind the younger hastati soldiers and the more experienced principes.

TRIBUNE OF THE PLEBEIANS – (aka plebeian tribunes) A plebeian tribune was a protector of the common people or plebeians. He had the power to veto legislation in the Senate and could introduce legislation as well. He could protect a plebeian from unjust punishment by a magistrate and prosecute and administer sentences.

TRIUMPH - A procession that was the highest honor bestowed upon a victorious general in the ancient Roman Republic; it was the summit of a Roman aristocrat's career. Triumphs were granted and paid for by the Senate and held in the city of Rome; although sometimes the victorious general would pay for his own. To triumph in Roman republican times a man was required to have been a general having complete command of the army and cavalry who had won a battle in the region he was assigned to, killing at least 5,000 of the enemy and ending the war. In the procession the general wore a toga with a purple stripe and rode in a chariot. The triumph began with a procession from the Triumphal Gate in the Campus Martius to the Temple of Jupiter on the Capitoline Hill, passing through the Forum and the Via Sacra along streets adorned with flowers and lined with people shouting, "Io triumphe!"

A general who did not earn a triumph might be granted an *ovation*, in which he walked or rode on horseback, wearing the purple-bordered toga of an ordinary magistrate and a wreath of myrtle.

VALERIUS - Publius Valerius Publicola (or Poplicola) came from the wealthy Valerii family of Sabine origin. He was one of four Roman patricians who were the leaders to overthrow the monarchy. He became a Roman consul along with his colleague Lucius Junius Brutus in 509 BC, which was considered to be the first year of the Roman Republic. His father was Volesus Valerius, and his brothers were Marcus Valerius Volesus and Manius Valerius Volesus Maximus. He had a daughter, Valeria, and possibly a son or grandson who was also named Publius Valerius Publicola who served as consul in 475 BC and 460 BC.

VESTAL VIRGINS - Vestal Virgins were young girls chosen between the ages of 6 and 10 by the Pontifex Maximus. They remained as virgins for 30 years. Afterward they could marry, but most chose to remain free. To be chosen as a Vestal Virgins you had to be of the required age, be freeborn and have respectable parents who were both alive, and have no physical or mental problems. Living in the House of the Vestal Virgins on the Roman Forum, near the Temple of Vesta, their duties included tending the perpetual fire in the Temple of Vesta, keeping their vow of chastity, fetching water from a sacred spring (they could not drink from the city water-supply system), preparing ritual food, caring for objects in the temple's inner sanctuary, and officiating at the Vestalia (June 7–15), the period of public worship of Vesta. Beatings were rendered for failure to attend to their duties. Breaking the vow of chastity was punished by being buried alive (the blood of a Vestal Virgin could not be spilled). The Vestal Virgins enjoyed privileges not open to married or single women of the same social status, which included freedom from their father's rule and the freedom to handle their own property.

VINEAE - The Romans preferred to assault enemy walls by building earthen ramps (*agger*) or simply scaling the walls with ladders. Soldiers working at the ramps were protected by shelters called *vineae*, that were arranged to form a long corridor. Convex wicker shields were used to form a screen to protect the front of the corridor during construction of the ramp.Soldiers were able to lift them and move them together in a row towards the enemy wall. They were covered with panels of woven twigs to give protection from archers. The roofs may have been reinforced with a double layer of timber boards to protect against large stones being hurled at them from above. The entire exterior would be covered with wetted animal skins to protect against fire arrows. The Romans were able to create protected galleries by joining several of these together. This enabled them to get close to outer walls and undermine them or build ramps up to them.

Made in United States
Orlando, FL
27 December 2024

56542057R00093